new directions FOR HIGHER EDUCATION

number 6
summer 1974

new directions for higher education

a quarterly sourcebook edited by
JB Lon Hefferlin

---

number 6
summer 1974

implementing field experience education

john duley
issue editor

Jossey-Bass Inc., Publishers
San Francisco · Washington · London

IMPLEMENTING FIELD EXPERIENCE EDUCATION
New Directions for Higher Education
Volume II, Number 2, Summer 1974
John Duley, Issue Editor

New Directions for Higher Education is published quarterly by Jossey-Bass, Inc., Publishers. Subscriptions are available at the regular rate for institutions, libraries, and agencies of $25 for one year. Individuals may subscribe at the special professional rate of $15 for one year. *New Directions* is numbered sequentially—please order extra copies by sequential number. The volume and issue numbers above are included for the convenience of libraries. Second-class postage rates paid at San Francisco, California, and at additional mailing offices.

Correspondence:
Subscriptions, single-issue orders, change of address notices, undelivered copies, and other correspondence should be sent to *New Directions* Subscriptions, Jossey-Bass, Inc., Publishers, 615 Montgomery Street, San Francisco, California 94111. Editorial correspondence should be sent to the Editor-in-Chief, JB Lon Hefferlin, at the same address.

Library of Congress Catalogue Card Number LC 74-2329

Cover design by Willi Baum
Manufactured in the United States of America

contents

editor's notes

This issue reviews the state of the art of field experience education. In this type of education, the primary focus of learning is activity undertaken in a particular off-campus setting under the sponsorship, but not the direct supervision, of a faculty member. In contrast, the traditional classroom educational experience emphasizes the predetermined syllabus, texts, lectures, and content to be mastered within the structured and controlled learning environment provided by the faculty member. Because of the diversity of situations utilized and purposes stated by those who are involved in field experience education it is difficult to describe it more precisely and still provide a definition which is capable of encompassing all the programs that are offered. Within the general field there are several different types of programs:

Cross-Cultural Experience. A student involves himself in another culture or subculture of his own society in a deep and significant way, either as a temporary member of a family, a worker in that society, or as a volunteer in a social agency, with the intention, as a participant observer, of learning as much as he can about that culture and his own.

Preprofessional Training. A student serves in assigned responsibilities under the supervision of a professional in the field of education, medicine, law, social work, nursing, or ministry, putting the theory he has learned into practice, gaining skills in the profession, and being evaluated by his supervisor.

Institutional Analysis/Career Exploration. "A student has a temporary period of supervised work that provides opportunities to develop skills, to test abilities and career interests, and to systematically examine institutional cultures in light of the central theoretical notions in a chosen academic field of study" (Zauderer, 1973, p. 1).

Work Experience (Cooperative Education). "Cooperative Education is that education plan which integrates classroom experience and practical work experience in industrial, business, government, or service-type work situations in the community. The work experience constitutes a regular and essential element in the educative process and some minimum amount of work experience and minimum standard of successful performance on the job are included in the requirements of the institution for a degree" (The National Commission for Cooperative Education, 1971).

Service-Learning Internship. "Service-learning has been defined as: the integration of the accomplishment of a task which meets human need with conscious educational growth. A service-learning internship is designed to provide students responsibility to meet a public need and a significant learning experience within a public or private institution for a specified period of time, usually 10 to 15 weeks" (Sigmon, 1972, p. 2).

Social/Political Action. A student secures a placement, under faculty sponsorship, which gives him the opportunity to be directly engaged in working for social change either through community organizing, political activity, research/action projects, or work with organizations seeking to bring about changes in the social order. He also usually fulfills a learning contract made with his faculty sponsor.

Personal Growth and Development. A student undertakes a program in an off-campus setting that is designed to further his personal growth and development, such as the wilderness survival programs of the Outward Bound Schools, or an apprenticeship to an artist or a craftsman, or residence in a monastery for the development of his spiritual life, or participation in an established group psychological or human relations program.

Field Research. A student undertakes an independent or group research project in the field under the supervision of a faculty member, applying the concepts and methods of an academic discipline such as geology, archaeology, geography, or sociology.

While not an exhaustive list, this covers most of the types of programs offered in colleges and universities as field experience education.

In the late 1960s and early 1970s, with the development of experimental, residential, and cluster colleges, field experience education programs expanded rapidly. Dr. James Feeney, who was then director of the Field Experience Program of New College, Sarasota, Florida, with the aid of the Bowman C. Lingle Trust, hosted a conference at New College in 1972 to explore the need for a formal organization of those involved in field experience education. As a result of that meeting the Society for Field Experience Education was formed. Its purposes are to encourage the development of field experience education, facilitate sharing of ideas and activities among institutions concerned with field experience, support exploration of issues in field education, and be a source of expertise for those seeking counsel regarding field experience programs and projects.

The papers in this issue were originally developed for the annual conference of the Society, which was held at Michigan State University on October 25-26, 1973. Their authors were asked to gather information from as many sources as they could, describe present practices, and develop some normative suggestions based on their investigation and their experience. The edited results of their work are offered with the hope that those engaged in field experience education, those anticipating involvement, those required to make administrative decisions affecting such programs, and those pursuing related new directions in higher education—for example, people who are developing competency-oriented degree programs and those seeking effective ways to assess prior learning acquired by nontraditional students entering or returning to the campus to complete baccalaureate work—will find this volume a useful resource.

We begin with descriptions of three programs which have very different purposes, clientele, and resources: an urban community college program serving predominantly "new students," a cross-cultural program of a liberal education college within a large state university, and a statewide service-learning internship program involving students from colleges and universities throughout the state. These descriptions are followed by papers dealing with the roles and responsibilities of the participants: students, faculty, agency supervisors, and campus administrators. Subsequent contributions examine ways to gain acceptance and support for this type of education, issues related to program development, methods of evaluation, and finally, information about additional resources.

Readers interested in learning more about The Society for Field Experience Education can contact the Society at 131 Snyder Hall, Justin Morrill College, Michigan State University, East Lansing, Michigan 48824. Individual membership in the Society is $2 for students and $10 for others. Institutional memberships are $50. The Society issues a newsletter three times a year, publishes occasional papers by its members, and conducts an annual conference—the next one scheduled for October 11-13, 1974, in Atlanta, Georgia. Further information about the conference is available from Mr. Mike Hart, Georgia Intern Program, State Capitol, Atlanta, Georgia 30334, or the Society's president, Dean Bernard Charles, Livingston College, Rutgers University, New Brunswick, New Jersey 08903.

John Duley
Issue Editor

references

National Commission for Cooperative Education. *Colleges, Universities and Community Colleges Offering Cooperative Education Programs.* New York: National Commission for Cooperative Education, 1971.

Sigmon, R. *A Notebook on Service Learning.* Raleigh: North Carolina Internship Office, October, 1972.

Zauderer, D. G. *Urban Internships in Higher Education.* ERIC/Higher Education Research Report No. 9. Washington, D.C.: The American Association of Higher Education, 1973.

An urban program combats second-best status and promotes self-discovery.

experiential education at a community college

l. steven zwerling

In her book about the so-called New Student in higher education K. Patricia Cross cites a survey in which new and "traditional" students were asked to dream about their futures: If you had your choice of anything in the world, what would you like to do? Seventy-eight percent of *new* female students dreamed of becoming typists and secretaries; 69 percent of *new* male students selected auto mechanic. Whereas 76 percent of *traditional* female students dreamed of becoming authors of novels, as did 59 percent of *traditional* male students. These are all highest choices for each of the four categories of students. Second and third choices are also revealing: new female–office clerk and beautician; new male–army officer and electrician; traditional female–high school teacher and college professor; traditional male–spaceman and college professor (Cross, 1971, p. 94).

New Students are defined primarily as children of blue-collar workers, usually the first in their family to attend college. They are low achievers in high school and likely to attend a local, publicly supported community college. Traditional students are those who have traditionally gone to college: they are fairly affluent, from families whose parents have had some college education, high achievers in high school and on tests such as the S.A.T., and likely to attend four-year public or private colleges and universities.

So if we were to establish internship or off-campus study programs for these two types of students based upon what Cross claims to be both their achievements and their aspirations, it would be a rather simple, clear-cut process: for the traditional student, set up field study that is both humanistic and preprofessional; for the New Student, set up off-campus work/study that is both specialized and prepractical.

But is this the best way to proceed? It is if we want to reinforce the current social order while promulgating an illusion of the rich possibilities for social mobility via universal higher education. However, if we want to help make the rhetoric that supports open access to higher education a functioning reality, we had better come up with learning structures that will enable New Students to rise within the society in ways that reflect their true potential.

A way of looking for the reality behind the rhetoric of open access and social mobility is to examine some of the differences between the explicit *and* hidden messages delivered by both open-door and selective colleges. Open-admissions colleges thrive on the belief that they offer low-achieving students another chance to "make it"; that is their explicit message. But the hidden message is that up to 75 percent of their students never complete two years; this creates an atmosphere of pervasive failure that seriously and negatively affects the chances of all who attend. Such dual messages may be found in off-campus study programs as well. One kind of hidden message, for example, is communicated by elite colleges' experiential programs that place prelaw students in pretigious law firms or in public interest legal work; the sponsoring college thus reveals how it regards itself and what it thinks are appropriate careers for its students. An open-door college's off-campus program that places its students in health technology work or in computer maintenance programs also subtly but powerfully shows how it perceives its functions and what is considered appropriate work for its students.

What is disturbing about these different messages is that an Antioch, which primarily serves "traditional" students, is likely to offer experiential work of the former kind whereas a community college, which serves New Students, is likely to offer the latter kinds of internships. And since to a substantial degree the Antiochs and the community colleges are stratified according to the socioeconomic status of their students, the structures of their off-campus programs contribute to the maintenance of existing social and economic differences rather than to their reduction. So the rhetoric that proclaims higher education for all (a community college's rhetoric) or that promotes higher education for the able regardless of race, class, or ethnicity (an Antioch's rhetoric) as an effective means of facilitating social mobility masks the reality of the way these different kinds of schools are structured. And since the essence of institutions is generally expressed in their every part, off-campus study components also reflect this conflict between rhetoric and reality: an Antioch is structured for the success of the students it carefully selects; a community college is structured for the selective failure of the students for whom it opens its doors.

an affective environment for motivation

What follows is a description of an integrated on- and off-campus learning structure that I feel serves the real potential of New Students. All of this is distilled from rather extensive experience at Staten Island Community College, one of those many places in America where these students come looking for their share of the Dream. Within our Experimental Program, as part of an integrated academic curriculum, we ask each of our first-semester students to join an Educational Development Seminar (E.D.S.). Examining and stimulating motivation is the function of the E.D.S. It meets once a week for an extended period of time and includes fifteen to twenty students and a faculty leader or facilitator. The objective of the E.D.S. initially is to help students understand how they got where they are, that their presence in a community college is at least as much the result of class, ethnicity, and the inadequacies of their prior schooling as it is the fault of their own inherent limitations.

This understanding helps build the self-confidence which is essential to making ambitious but strategically sound plans for their future education and careers. Perhaps for the first time in their lives, E.D.S. students begin to take control of their own education and hence their own destiny. When they begin to see a new career goal as realizable, the problems of English Composition or Biology 100 or Math 15 become just that—problems to be solved. No longer are they insurmountable barriers. Students begin to see the difficulties of acquiring verbal and mathematical skills as important but minor battles in a larger struggle.

In these basic skills most community college students start considerably behind many traditional college students. Various forms of college-level compensatory or remedial education have failed. Projected dropout and failure rates for the City University of

New York's community college Open Admissions students run as high as 80 percent during their first two college years (Rempson, 1972, p. 12). To close the large gaps in reading, math, and writing, often at least 4 or 5 years' worth, dramatic breakthroughs are required. Gaining 8 or 10 months in measured reading skill in 5 months is hardly good enough. We have found that partly as the result of the powerful motivation generated in our E.D.S.'s these breakthroughs regularly occur.

The E.D.S. frequently begins with an exercise designed to help a student trace the contours of his/her educational biography. The initial question often is: What is your first memory of school? As the members of the group track these down and begin to discover the connections between their early experiences and their current situation they begin to relate to each other in an intense and open manner. This atmosphere of honesty and sharing is essential to the success of the Seminar. Faculty members must demonstrate equal candor. We too must explore our educational and career histories; we must check to see whether we too feel that community colleges are second-rate institutions and that teaching in one makes us second-rate people. It is virtually impossible to try to help people understand their educational histories and to make plans for themselves if we ourselves are not involved in the same process.

One of the lessons of the E.D.S. is that our dreams and aspirations in part result from the society within us (Berger, 1963); the implication is that unless we understand this and, if we choose, intervene in this process, our future attainments also are sociologically rather predictable. Therefore, part of what we do is help students shape their own educational and career plans. If they wish, we try to help them develop their own plan to confront society's. Plans include components of traditional academic advisement (What courses should I take? To which college should I transfer?), personal counseling (Is smoking dope a problem? What do your parents think of all this?), financial aid advisement (Is applying for financial aid the same as going on welfare? Is it a good idea to take out a loan?). But the approach is holistic, and it also frequently advocates the student rather than the institution.

Unless the E.D.S. begins with the way we *feel* about our own histories and goes from affective exploration to cognitive and rational understanding, it is no more than a new version of a familiar academic exercise. The new directions proposed here assume a powerful affective environment that often goes unacknowledged but which must, as with the social and political roles of schools, be made explicit in order to aid the release of our students' potential. If, for example, the bookstore refuses to stock anything other than required texts and school sweatshirts, it teaches students something about how the college regards their academic potential. This affective environment must either be changed or, at the least, students must learn to perceive its hidden messages and thus protect themselves against its effects.

Another important function of affective learning is to help our students validate their own prior experiences. The academic world reflects upper-middle-class values and values upper-middle-class culture. Lower-class people feel put down or alienated by this kind of exclusive collegiate environment. Validating working-class culture via affective learning in community college does not mean a different kind of exclusiveness (although at times I see this happening at Staten Island, encouraged by a misdirected radicalism): it means a cultural balance within which all people can have a chance to feel good about themselves.

self-discovery through work experience

How, specifically, does off-campus study fit into all of this? As students begin to feel they have it within themselves to become whatever reflects their real abilities, as their basic skills improve, they are ready to work for credit at an internship. We do not see internships primarily either as job training or as exercises in how to be responsible on the job—although some of this is inevitably involved. Rather we see internships as part of our more fundamental educational objectives: encouraging self-examination and self-definition. They are a means to help make real for community college students the possibility of becoming, say, a teacher by offering close contact with the school world. Perhaps a student will work at a teacher's side in a municipal high school where he/she can learn at close range that teachers are just people. Institutional structures are such that prior to this experience our student interns have virtually never known or spoken to teachers except as students. Cultural structures are such that few community college students have encountered teachers in noninstitutional settings. If via the co-professional structure of our internship program students can come to demystify teachers and begin to perceive them as *people* with both skills and limitations, then perhaps, if they choose, our students can become teachers.

As part of the larger process of self-definition we encourage students to sample a variety of different internships—sometimes as many as three or four during the course of a year. We encourage this because we have come to learn that at first our students are reluctant to reveal their real dreams and aspirations. They have in the past frequently experienced failure and have learned to live with drastically limited notions of success and with thwarted expectations. To say "teacher" is tempting but still often risky after only one semester at Staten Island. There have been many instances in which students initially work at auto mechanic internships and then after a few weeks or months come in to tell us that they would really prefer to work with a high school history teacher. At that point we immediately help them change internships rather than insisting that they wait until the beginning of a new semester. When the moment of redefinition comes, we must be able to help students act at that moment. I hasten to add that not all changes represent upward movement within the status hierarchy. And that is all to the good if these changes *also* represent choices arrived at as freely and with as little social pressure as possible.

We had one student, for example, who expressed interest in working in a high-status position behind the scenes in the communications media, as a director or producer, but during one year he dramatically "lowered" his aspirational level. He went from work in a film studio to an off-campus job at a "radical" radio station (he became disillusioned when they treated him "like garbage" because of his lowly position—an apparent contradiction of their professed egalitarianism), to production work at the American Broadcasting Company's "College Scoreboard" program, and then finally to rather low-status work as a paramedic for the New York City Police Department. He loves the work and is doing brilliantly. His experience represents a real choice independent of social and parental pressures.

internship seminars

These kinds of changes are both facilitated and monitored within another Educational Development Seminar that runs concurrently with the off-campus work itself. (Incidentally, to fit realistically within the school, work, and commuting schedule of community college students, we set up internships on a one-work-day-per-week basis.) In this E.D.S., again comprising fifteen to twenty interns with a faculty leader, students continue to shape or alter their plans in the light of what they learn from their work and other academic experiences. Without this Seminar the desire to switch internships might reflect whimsy more than meaningful self-examination or thoughtful redefinition. Interesting work-related questions frequently arise. If, for example, the interns perceive the callousness with which public schools frequently treat their students, what can they do about it as mere community college interns? Do they confront the administration, demanding they act more humanely? Do they stifle their anger for the sake of keeping their job? Do they quit in frustration? These are real problems that have much to do with what it is to be a teacher.

In one Internship E.D.S. I worked with that was specifically set up for teaching interns, we tried to deal with some of these questions through role-playing exercises. One student was troubled by what she felt to be the inhuman way in which the teacher with whom she was working treated her third-grade class. This teacher felt her students were, in her words, "animals" (they were the lowest track third-grade class); and according to our student, Cathy, the class' wild behavior was beginning to convince her that the teacher was right. But she was troubled because as part of our E.D.S. she had read *Summerhill* and Herbert Kohl and John Holt, and similar critics, whose analyses of the "wild" behavior of children in schools tended to indict the institution rather than the students. But still Cathy's experience was creating the kind of frustration and bitterness that was turning her against the children. She felt she was beginning to resemble the familiar bitter fifty-year-old New York City schoolteacher after only a month on the job. She was miserable. To try to test who was right, the third-grade teacher or John Holt, we had Cathy role play first the teacher she was working with and then a John Holt-style teacher. The rest of us played the students. In addition to enabling us to reconnect with our own third-grade experiences, the exercises helped Cathy see how different classroom structures and different teacher expectations dramatically affect the classroom environment. Obviously not all the problems evaporated; but she did see that when she allowed a certain structured disorder, when she stopped pursuing an unrelenting sense of discipline and order, the children began to become responsive to classroom learning. Cathy continued to work at the school and got the teacher to agree to allow her to work privately with five of the most "hopeless" students. The assistant principal found Cathy an unused book storage closet, and she began to try to apply some of her own methods. It wasn't easy and by no means did she achieve miracles. But her students' reading scores showed a measurable improvement and they stopped behaving like "animals," at least with Cathy.

Also in these Internship E.D.S.'s we examine the concept of

work itself. Many students today are rejecting or at least questioning the Protestant ethic which teaches one to seek life-affirming satisfaction through work. One part of their culture would like work to be neither essential nor inevitable; life-affirming satisfactions should be sought in various ways. But they learn, partly through their internships, that the world of work is still basically structured according to the older ethic; and so for these students, particularly, unless bridges can be built between the old ethic and the new, schooling remains irrelevant.

One way of at least locating the foundations for these bridges is to help students discover specific kinds of work that reflect the new ethic. Community college students, who come primarily from working-class and lower-middle-class backgrounds, have a rather circumscribed view of the world of work. They usually perceive work to be an unrelenting dreary struggle for inadequate wages. They are generally unaware of some of the newer, more exotic, perhaps more satisfying work situations. One student, committed to the new work ethic, was about to drop out of school because everything Staten Island had to offer seemed inevitably to lead to a "straight," nine-to-five, jacket-and-tie kind of job. But as a result of a series of internships that began in a photography studio and ended with his working at the Sierra Club, he discovered that one might both make a living and find satisfaction doing conservation work. He did so well at the Sierra Club, provoking them to get interested in fighting to preserve a wilderness area in eastern Canada, that they encouraged him to apply to Syracuse University's School of Forestry. Their letters of recommendation helped him gain admission with a large financial aid package.

placement

In addition to structuring an off-campus work/study program flexible enough so that as students go through the process of self-definition they can serve a variety of internships that relate to their personal changes, we have found it valuable *not* to offer up a menu of work/study opportunities as is common at many colleges. What we do instead, as much as possible, is individualize our placements: when a student tells us that he/she wants to work in a psychiatric setting we spend a considerable amount of time in first helping the student define as specifically as he/she can just what kind of work he/she is seeking. Of course we often present various options drawn from experience, but the focus is always on helping students define and refine their preferences. This method is related to our objective of having students learn the skills necessary to take control of their lives. Control is related to choice. A preselected shopping list of internships limits choice. Our individualized approach, we feel, is limited only by the students' growing strength and imagination.

To help this process, obviously, we also need an internship director of equal strength and imagination. This person has to be a teacher (nonclassroom) as well as a procurer of placements. This person has to be aware of the overall objectives of the program and reinforce these by the manner in which he/she works with students. Our director of internships is sensitive to the idea that his role is to facilitate choosing rather than to direct or control it. In addition to the lengthy talks he has with students as they go about trying to define their futures, he often gets them involved in seeking out and setting up internships themselves. This takes more time. Sometimes it also means that we lose potential internship sites because students aren't as effective in setting them up as is our director. It would obviously be easier for him to pick up the telephone and set something up in the Anthropology Department of New York's Museum of Natural History, but if students can make this contact it demystifies our director's all-powerful image and reinforces the students' sense of their own growing confidence and strength. So we try to get them involved in the entire process and gladly risk whatever confusion or untidiness results from trying to help them gain control of their lives. Obviously, this doesn't always work and we have to pull out the menu, but it's worth the effort.

Something else is important that should be apparent from the examples of specific internships I have cited: A.B.C. Sports, Sierra Club, the Museum of Natural History. These are all "quality" internships, the best possible placements. As with everything else, there's a hidden message here, though we try to make it explicit: nothing but the best for our students. People accustomed to second best begin to think of themselves as second best. This is the usual experience for most of our students. We would as much as possible like to reverse this, not to turn the tables in the society but rather to help our people develop a positive sense of self-worth. And helping them find quality internships facilitates this development. After watching the Olympics on television Danny told us that, *although it was impossible,* he would like to work with the Wide World of Sports people. It was the "although it was impossible" that we were concerned about, not that we couldn't set it up but that Danny believed it was impossible for him. After all, he was just a community college student with a 2.6 gradepoint average. And although Danny only remained at A.B.C. for a short time, moving on to paramedical work after a couple of months, the process of helping him understand why he felt it was impossible as well as his helping in significant ways to set up the placement taught him a great deal about his power and worth that should be valuable to him in whatever he does in the future.

There is another by-product to this type of placement. When we first contacted A.B.C., and many other places, they too thought it was impossible to work with community college students. They too believed community colleges and their students were second best. If they had allowed students to work with them in the past, the interns had always been, for example, Antioch students. Their notion initially was that the proper kind of internship for community college students might be to help maintain and repair A.B.C.'s computers or air conditioners. So in addition to working with Danny's image of himself we also had to work with A.B.C.'s image of Danny. If left unexamined and unchallenged, both could contribute to defeating Danny. And again if left unacknowledged or unsaid, the way places such as A.B.C. operate communicates a hidden message that is more powerful than the overt but less honest message printed at the bottom line of their Help Wanted advertisements: "We are an equal opportunity employer."

How the type and quality of an internship communicate can be seen dramatically in another example from a couple of years ago. In fact this incident had a great deal to do with shaping the development of our internship program at Staten Island. During the first year of Open Admissions in the City University of New York (1970-1971), I was the director of our Preparatory Skills Program at S.I.C.C. Toward the end of that year I was talking with Brian, one of our brightest students, about his plans for the summer. He told me how difficult it was to find jobs but that he had solid leads at a supermarket and at a gas station. I knew he was interested in college teaching or administration and asked how these summer jobs related to that aspiration. Obviously, he told me, only in that they would bring some money—certainly not in his day-to-day work. While talking with him I remembered a job from the summer before that a Yale sophomore, Mike, had secured for himself. Mike was also interested in college teaching and administration, and when he went to the Yale Placement Office to look for help, they set him up for the summer working as an intern in the office of the President of S.I.C.C., William Birenbaum. Not only did he get paid rather handsomely but he was also able to earn academic credit. And when I thought about the different way Brian would spend his summer it made me furious. After discussing all of this at great length, we decided it would be a good idea for Brian to see our placement counselor to find out what kinds of things she had to offer. He also decided that when she asked him what he wanted to do for the summer he would tell her he wanted to work for Kingman Brewster, president of Yale. The fact that when Brian came up with this idea we both laughed about it for ten minutes also taught us something about the differences between Yale and S.I.C.C. and how those differences have affected all of us. He did go to our placement counselor and the few openings she had were for stock clerk jobs at Sears and the like. When he told her about wanting to work for Kingman Brewster she looked at him as if he were literally crazy. Well, Brian did get "crazy" about this. He learned via these covert messages what S.I.C.C. was expecting of him and became determined to do something about it. He didn't go to Yale for the summer but did get to go there to take some courses the following spring semester. He finished his B.A. in three years—just about unheard of for an Open Admissions student. He has just been admitted to Columbia University's Ph.D. program in anthropology with a large fellowship.

Obviously a few examples are not infinitely generalizable, but at S.I.C.C. through the years we have had significantly more than just a few Cathys, Dannys, and Brians. It is becoming clear that by putting the hidden curriculum to work for students in egalitarian ways, by building an off-campus work/study program to release rather than to contain potential, schooling, even at the college level, can in fact serve notions of equality. The problem with Christopher Jencks and others is that they haven't perceived that the social history of schools has unfortunately been to *serve* notions of inequality. Some of us at S.I.C.C. feel that we have begun to find some ways to reverse this process.

references

Berger, P. *Invitation to Sociology*. New York: Anchor Books, 1963.

Cross, K. P. *Beyond the Open Door.* San Francisco: Jossey-Bass, 1971.

Rempson, J. "Minority Access to Higher Education in New York City." *The City Almanac.* New York, Center for New York City Affairs of the New School for Social Research, 1972, 7 (2).

L. Steven Zwerling is director of one of Staten Island Community College's experimenting inner colleges. Prior to that he directed S.I.C.C.'s Open Admissions Program. He co-produces and co-hosts a weekly radio program in New York City on WRVR called "Education on the Line." He is the author of Second Best: The Community College's Commitment to Failure.

Justin Morrill's program is described in detail, including objectives, preparation of students, follow-up, and evaluation.

cross-cultural field study

john duley

Justin Morrill College is a four-year, degree-granting college of Michigan State University providing a bachelor of arts degree in liberal education. The purpose of the college is to help students become effective and humane autonomous learners. It does this through allowing students to become heavily involved in designing their own education, college governance, peer advising, and student-faculty interaction. Also included in the plan of education is a pass-no credit written evaluation system and a field of concentration designed by the student and faculty advisor consisting of at least one year's work in upper-division courses taken outside the college in any of the departments or colleges of the University.

Another distinctive feature of the college is the Field Study Program in which students spend a term off campus in a cross-cultural learning experience of their own choosing. In this program, which is a requirement for graduation, students arrange their own placements using information provided by the office and by the Center for Alternatives in and to Higher Education of the United Ministries in Higher Education. Students choose from three types of experiences:

1. *Cross-Cultural Learning.* Students involve themselves in

other cultures or subcultures as temporary members of families, as workers, or as volunteers in social agencies with the intention of learning as much as possible about those cultures as participant-observers.

2. *Preprofessional Experience.* Students test out professions through field study experiences in social work, teaching, law, or medicine by serving as paraprofessionals.

3. *Social Action Involvement.* Students locate or design experiences which give them the opportunity to be directly involved in working for social change through community organizing, research/action projects, or organizations seeking to bring about change in the social order.

To be approved a project must meet certain criteria. First, the project must provide for active participation in the daily life and affairs of a social environment new to the student. Second, the project must be at least nine weeks long. Third, if it is in a foreign country, the student must have a two-year competency in the language. And last, arrangements must be nearly finalized before a staff member will permit the student to enroll for credit.

The objectives of the program are for students to develop and demonstrate the following skills:

1. *Information Source Development:* The ability to use many information sources within a social environment. The student should, therefore, develop information-gathering skills such as observing, questioning associates and chance acquaintances, and listening with care.

2. *Cultural Understanding:* Awareness and understanding of the structures and the values, feelings, and attitudes of people in another culture and the ways these influence behavior.

3. *Interpersonal Communication:* The ability not only to listen well and speak clearly but also to be sensitive to nonverbal communication, such as the messages available from physical movements, facial expressions, and the quality of face-to-face encounter.

4. *Commitment to Persons and Relationships:* The ability to become involved deeply with people, to be able to give and inspire trust and confidence, to care and take action with and for them in accordance with one's concerns.

5. *Decision Making:* The ability to come to conclusions and take action in spite of inadequate, unreliable, and conflicting information. In making decisions in a cross-cultural setting a person must learn to trust feelings, searching for the best possible course or the most viable alternative.

6. *Self-Understanding:* Awareness of and insight into one's own learning processes, strengths, weaknesses, successes, failures, prejudices, values, emotions, and goals.

7. *Self-Reliance:* Independence, autonomy, resiliency, willingness to accept responsibility for one's actions and education, receptiveness to new experiences and ideas, confidence in one's self and ability to function independently.

8. *Written Communication:* The ability to communicate the impact of the field study experience, including knowledge of another culture, self-knowledge, and the changes, if any, that the experience brought about in the student's attitudes, values, interests, goals, beliefs, or convictions.

The purpose of the Field Study Program is not to insist that everyone be highly trained in these skills before departure, nor to insist that students attain a specified level of competence in them before credit will be awarded. Our purpose is to help the student further develop these skills. We believe that at this time in a person's life, development of these abilities is most effectively facilitated by helping students place themselves in circumstances of their own choosing where they must use these skills in order to accomplish their purposes; by requiring them to become conscious of occasions on which these skills are brought into play and the way in which they acted under those circumstances; and by giving students the opportunity with others who have had similar experiences to reflect on their experiences in a structured way.

the means of structured reflection

We have adapted John Flanagan's Critical Incident Technique (C.I.T.) for our program. The C.I.T. was an outgrowth of studies in the Aviation Psychology Program of the U.S. Army Air Force in World War II. The immediate purpose of the development of C.I.T. was to provide a basis for the selection and classification of air crews. Its successful use in analyzing such qualities as disorientation in pilots and combat leadership resulted in its extension and further development after the war. John Flanagan defines a "critical incident" as "any observable human activity that is sufficiently complete in itself to permit inferences and predictions to be made about the person performing the act. To be critical, an incident must occur in a situation where the purpose or intent of the act seems fairly clear to the observer and where its consequences are sufficiently definite to leave little doubt concerning its effects" (Flanagan,

1954, p. 327). We require each student to describe in a brief and concise manner nine incidents in which he attempted to use one of the identified cross-cultural education skills during his Field Study. Our adaptation of C.I.T. is essentially a procedure for gathering information concerning behavior in a defined situation. It consists of recording specific behaviors that are critical to the evaluation of an activity. The assumption underlying this technique is that reporting facts (incidents) regarding behavior is preferable to collecting interpretations, ratings, and opinions of others. Our adaptation is best seen in the "Guide to Critical Incident Writing" that we developed for use by our students. (See the following page.)

preparation seminar

Each student is required to participate in a five- to six-week seminar during the term prior to his Field Study. The purposes of this seminar are to improve the students' skills in making and recording observations; train them in "critical incident writing" and initiate the keeping of journals; introduce them to disorienting experiences that occur in strange cultures; introduce them to skills needed in information source development; introduce them to self-initiated learning contracts; and give them experience in using values clarification processes.

In order to accomplish these purposes the preparation seminar meets for one and a half hours each week and for a Saturday and includes the following components: orientation to the program's objectives and the bases for evaluation, instruction in critical incident writing and assignment of three incidents to be described, a day in the field, a follow-up discussion of the techniques they used, simulation of culturally disorienting experiences, value clarification exercises, development and use of individualized learning contracts for the last five weeks of the term, a paper at the end of the term in which the students describe their projects and their personal hopes and expectations regarding them, and a progress report on the learning contracts.

The day in the field is the first Saturday following the beginning of the Seminar. It provides students with a microcosm experience of functioning in a new environment. Students learn to use their own imaginations to try out various means of learning about a new community. The day also illustrates what insights can be developed and implications drawn from data gathered by various methods of studying a community. It acquaints students with a wide

Guide to Critical Incident Writing

A "critical incident" is a brief description of an event in which a student has sought to use one of the cross-cultural education skills. It should answer most of the following questions:

Which skill is the incident related to?

What was at issue: problem to be solved, decision to be made, action to be taken, mission to be accomplished, controversy to be settled, opinion to be arrived at, agreement or understanding to be reached.

What were the circumstances surrounding the event which are important to it: place, occasion, social contexts, time of day, weather.

Who were the people (significant factors about them): age, occupation, sex, attitudes, nature of involvement, relationships between the principals, emotions or feelings experienced.

What other information would help make the circumstances more understandable?

Behavior: Specifically what did you do (described in detail) in attempting to use the skill in the above circumstances?

Analysis:

A. Indicate in what ways this was a successful or unsuccessful demonstration of the skill.

B. Write a summary statement describing the following for the skill used:

1. *Information source development.* Summarize the process you went through in developing your information source or network.

2. *Cultural understanding.* What understanding or insights into that culture or your own did this incident give you?

3. *Interpersonal communication* and

4. *Commitment to persons and relationships.* Summarize the developmental process in the communication or the development of commitment.

5. *Decision making.* Summarize, in so far as possible, the information source development which took place, the alternatives and consequences you considered, your values which influenced the decision and what kind of decision-making strategy you were engaged in.

6. *Self-understanding.* Summarize the insight about yourself which the incident provided, including the values and goals which became clarified.

7. *Self-reliance.* Summarize how the incident helped you develop more self-reliance.

range of methods that can be used in learning about a new community after they have tried it on their own, and they gain knowledge about their own feelings and attitudes while in a new environment.

Students know only that they will be dropped off in a small Michigan community (population 500 to 5000) at around 9:00 a.m. on a Saturday morning and picked up again around 4:00 p.m. The instructions given to the students are to learn as much about that community as they can in a day's time, to decide for themselves what is important to learn in order to understand the community, and to use their own imaginations in designing strategies. They bring lunch money and decide, on their own, what clothing is most appropriate for the task and consistent with their life style.

At the end of the day, they meet in groups of no more than fifteen for a debriefing session in which they each report. All efforts to give direction to this session and to limit the reporting to significant learnings or the development of generalizations have proven ineffective. The students have personal stories to tell and no amount of effort to direct the discussion will divert them from telling their stories fully. Reflection does not seem possible at this time. This comes later in the written reports and in the descriptions of the critical incidents of the day. The students begin the day with considerable apprehension and complete it with sighs of relief and, in some cases, elation. Telling the story is a necessary completion of the experience.

The staff has personal conferences with the students during the following week. In these conferences, the first critical incidents and the day in the field reports are discussed. Also discussed are the feelings the students experienced and the effect their attitudes toward the day had on the learnings that took place. In the subsequent meeting of the seminar, the students describe the techniques they used in learning about their communities. These techniques are then compared with those used by sociologists and anthropologists.

For many students who have excellent track records academically, but have had little experience beyond what schooling has provided, the day in the field is often described almost as a rite-of-passage. In the written evaluations of the program the students, with few exceptions, indicate the day in the field was the most valuable part of the preparation seminar.

the field experience

Most of our students do their field study during the summer, although any of the four terms of the year is acceptable. Sixty percent of our students do their field study in a foreign country. One very significant element in this program is that it is an experience undertaken by a student alone and not as a member of a group. When two or more students undertake such experiences together we have found that they can and do lean on each other and do not enter into the new setting as fully as they would were they alone. For this reason we seldom approve projects that involve more than one student. (For examples of the placements our students arrange see the article on the Role of the Student.)

the follow-up seminar

When the students return to the campus they participate in follow-up seminars that meet weekly for five to six weeks. They turn in their nine critical incident descriptions to the seminar leader, having developed three of them in a full autobiographical style. A personal conference is scheduled with each student after the staff member has read the critical incident reports. In the conference the staff person assists the student in selecting one incident which the student presents orally to the follow-up seminar. The purpose of the presentation is to describe the experience and discuss its significance for the student. Following the presentation another student in the seminar conducts an interview. The purpose of this in-class interview is to help identify and clarify the values influencing the student's behavior in the incident and to facilitate the discussion of the significance of the field experience for the student. The student interviewer has the following list of questions as suggestions and develops his own on the basis of the presentation.

Interview Questions

1. Did you enjoy this experience/incident? Were you proud of it? Why?

2. Was there risk involved? What risk? What enabled you to take the risk? Why did you take it?

3. What other solutions, actions, alternatives were available to you? Why did you reject them?

4. Was your behavior consistent with the usual patterns of your life? If not, how is it inconsistent? Does it represent a new development or direction for you?

5. If values are involved, how did you determine that values were operating and how did you determine which values in particular?

6. What is significant about this incident?

7. What else about your field study leads you to believe this incident is indicative of "something significant"?

There are ten to twelve students in each follow-up seminar and with two oral presentations each week it lasts five to six weeks. By the end of its meetings a first draft of a final paper is due. This paper is a serious reflection on the student's experience. He draws conclusions regarding his learnings about himself, his culture, the culture he was in, and reports any changes that occurred in his values, attitudes, career or educational plans, interests or concerns. In writing the paper, he uses the critical incident reports and his journal as supportive evidence for his conclusions. The critique of the first draft is returned and the student reworks it for final submission by the end of the term.

evaluation

Both the student and the program are evaluated. The assessment of the student is a written Pass-No Credit evaluation completed on a form which contains the following information given to the student in the Preparation Seminar: a paragraph describing the three-term nature of Field Study, Preparation Seminar, term in the field, and Follow-Up Seminar, and the work expected of the student in each phase. Directly beneath this paragraph, on the left-hand half of the page, are listed the seven cross-cultural objectives of the course and the objective of writing competence. On the right-hand side of the page, directly opposite each of the objectives, are stated the bases of evaluation which will be used by the instructor. For example:

Objectives:	*Bases of Evaluation:*
Demonstrated ability in:	
1. Information Source Development	1. Day in the Field, field experience, critical incident descriptions, final paper.

Blank space is left on the form for the faculty member to indicate the quality of the student's performance in demonstrating competence in the cross-cultural education skills.

The evaluator uses the evaluation written by the staff member who had the student in the Preparation Seminar, the written work from that seminar, the nine critical incident reports, the oral presentation, and the final paper. Given the clarity of the program objectives, as well as the quantity and quality of feedback from the student, the written evaluation is fairly easy to do and usually has the specificity one looks for in good letters of recommendation.

The evaluation of the program done by each student is a

four-part, six-page semantics differential questionnaire that asks the student to indicate:

(1) the learning opportunities that were available to him through this experience (not how well he used them);

(2) the consequences of the Field Experience;

(3) his evaluation of the Field Study Program (five questions requiring a written answer asking for suggestions regarding changes and what aspects of the program were of greatest help);

(4) his personal objectives in the Field Study and whether they were realized.

We are also using the Allport, Vernon, Lindzey "Study of Values" and Milton Rokeach's "Survey of Values" for pre and post tests but have not used them long enough to be able to report our findings.

reference

Flanagan, J. "The Critical Incident Technique," *Psychological Bulletin.* 1954, *51* (4), 327-358.

John Duley is assistant professor and director of the Field Study Program of Justin Morrill College at Michigan State University. He served on the original steering committee which founded the Society for Field Experience Education and was the chairperson of the Society's 1973 Conference. He is also the director of the college's Venture Fund Project, a competency oriented degree program for nontraditional students.

The North Carolina Internship Office has an operational objective to establish a network of programs which extend opportunities for service-learning to students enrolled in the forty-five senior public and private colleges in the state.

service-learning in north carolina

robert sigmon

The idea of service-learning internships as practiced in North Carolina is in part a utopian vision.* Participants, through combining service on behalf of others with personal educational growth, are challenged to consider the possibilities of a service-learning life style; learn how to learn through experience; strengthen their cultural commitments; and hone skills of goal-setting, interpersonal relations, and work competencies.

The service-learning experiential education model is also an institutional change strategy. Colleges and universities are confronted with the option of expanding learning environments to include public and human need settings beyond the classroom and library. Public organizations are confronted with the possibilities of

*Service-learning is defined as the integration of the accomplishment of a public task with conscious educational growth. A typical service-learning internship is a ten- to fifteen-week full-time activity in which students carry out planned work and learning tasks, receive financial remuneration and academic credit. For an elaboration of the service-learning model, see North Carolina Internship Office, 1972.

using inexpensive manpower resources and creating learning opportunities for young people.

With these rather humanitarian, political, and educational assumptions, the Southern Regional Education Board (SREB) and the State of North Carolina initiated a process in 1969 "to increase the number of opportunities for students to have internship experiences with state and local agencies and other organizations in the state concerned with social and economic development."

In 1971, the General Assembly of North Carolina appropriated funds for "increasing the utilization of students as manpower, for developing public needs as learning environments for senior college students, and for testing the service-learning experiential education model."

The North Carolina Internship Office (NCIO), the agent created to provide program development, technical assistance and informational support for these purposes, has an operational objective to establish a network of programs which will extend opportunities for service-learning to students enrolled in the forty-five senior public and private colleges in the state. The NCIO is jointly sponsored by the University of North Carolina General Administration and the State Government Department of Administration. This dual sponsorship symbolizes the coming together of service and learning activities advocated by NCIO.

NCIO functions and style

With this goal of developing a network of programs, undergirded by the assumptions of service-learning, NCIO staff functions focused on fund raising, encouraging colleges and public agencies to create service-learning programs, and information exchange from 1969 to 1972. Undergraduate programs were initiated on twelve campuses; special issue programs, involving students with planning, environmental, legal, and health assignments, were created; and urban models were assisted in Charlotte, Winston-Salem, and Greensboro.

A recent Southern Regional Education Board (SREB) evaluation noted NCIO's distinctive style of operation.

> First, the NCIO respects the autonomy of the academic institutions and public agencies with which it works. The NCIO serves as a counselor and an advocate of service-learning, concentrating its efforts on building a commitment to service-

> learning and helping the institution incorporate service-learning into its curriculum. Second, the NCIO is flexible and pragmatic. It is open to the needs and interests of the agencies and institutions with which it works. Third, the NCIO maintains a low profile. It seeks to do its work in such a way as to emphasize the achievement of the various programs it assists [1973, p. 6].

NCIO has not been a program, but an enabler of college and agency based programs for student involvement.

results

Service-learning programs have been most successfully developed at Mars Hill College, Appalachian State University, UNC-Charlotte, UNC-Greensboro, and Pembroke State University. In each location, relationships between the higher education institutions and area public agencies have been developed. In these institutions and in many others, the key question has become "What's the limit within a baccalaureate degree for experiential education credits?" when it once was "What are the reasons for having experiential learning programs?"

NCIO staff members have prepared, printed, and distributed more than thirty reports, studies, and films related to student involvement with service-learning activities.

Being physically located within a major department of state government, the NCIO provided leadership among state agencies for creating and maintaining student involvement programs during 1972 and 1973. Through encouraging departments to consider the use of students, a network of individuals evolved who developed a climate which led Governor Jim Holshouser, on April 10, 1973, to announce: "As a matter of policy, the Governor and the Department of Administration encourage the fullest use of students to achieve an increased productivity of state government departments and to provide distinctive public service-learning opportunities for young citizens of North Carolina." The governor created a Student Internship Advisory Council to plan for and coordinate service-learning internship opportunities among state agencies. A staff coordinator was appointed in January 1974 and year-round programming is now under way for student service-learning within state government. In relation to state government programs NCIO now functions as cheerleader and advisor.

research activities

With the creation of new service-learning programs around the state, the brokerage role of NCIO has been complemented by a research role. David Kiel, a doctoral student at the University of North Carolina at Chapel Hill, conducted studies in 1970, 1971, and 1972 designed to describe "what was happening in service-learning internships." The culmination of these studies resulted in a report, "Student Learning Through Community Involvement" (available from Student Internship Program, SREB, Atlanta). Four major benefits were noted for student learning:

1. Students develop more hopeful, knowledgeable, and concerned attitudes toward community problem-solving.
2. Students experience an increased motivation to work and learn in public need settings after learning to work effectively with others in internships.
3. Students learn a great deal about their personal abilities and cultural commitments.
4. There is an immediate impact on the students' behavior and on their plans for the future.

Heather Hoose, a student research assistant with NCIO during the spring and summer of 1973, conducted a follow-up study of fifty-six former service-learning interns who had been supported by SREB and NCIO initiated efforts between 1967 and 1971. An interpretation of her data (see Hoose, 1973), based on interviews and questionnaires, is that the service-learning experiential education model does foster a service-learning life style (over 50 percent of the students questioned are now in public service jobs); create a new awareness about how to learn through experience; provide settings for examining cultural values; and assist with personal skill development. A further interpretation suggests that the service-learning experiential education model offers education and manpower policy makers a rich alternative for responding to the needs of older youth for learning opportunities in public need settings.

While developing and evaluating service-learning programs, the NCIO staff generated data about other kinds of community-based experiential education. During the 1971-1972 academic year, an inventory of the forty-five senior colleges and twelve private junior colleges identified 308 programs placing more than sixteen thousand students in community-based learning programs sanctioned by the institutions. Nine categories of programs emerged, with service-learning programs as one category.

SREB's recent organizational review of NCIO accomplishments concludes with this statement:

> The North Carolina Internship Office has accomplished much in its four years of operation. Off-campus service-learning opportunities in North Carolina's colleges and universities have greatly enriched the educational process and, at the same time, allowed students to be involved in the solution of social, economic and governmental problems in the state. NCIO's accomplishments are seen by the staff of SREB's Student Intern Project as significant not only for the State of North Carolina but for higher education generally. The NCIO can serve as a model for students, educators, public officials and others concerned about having higher education relate more closely to the issues and problems of our society and ways to make more effective use of resources [1973, pp. 23-24].

student-originated options

Not content to rest on the knowledge that service-learning internships offer richly textured learning alternatives in the state and that curricular offerings are changing on many campuses, NCIO in 1973 began worrying about "what constitutes appropriate responses to the needs of youth for public involvement responsibilities and for educational alternatives in public need settings?" Going somewhat beyond the worrying stage, NCIO initiated two programs designed to expand the use of the service-learning experiential education model.

With Appalachian Regional Commission and Bicentennial funds, student-originated service-learning internship programs were developed. An Appalachian area program involved seventy-four students in self-initiated development and learning projects (a detailed report is available from the NCIO). Student-originated projects within Bicentennial themes have involved twenty-one students in activities ranging from researching preblues black banjo music in the Carolinas to intensive study of an isolated Southern mill town. In each project, students completed a thorough application process which became the basis for developing contracts between the NCIO and the individual students. Student-originated service-learning internships are designed primarily to place major responsibility for doing and learning on the students.

With Coastal Plains Regional Commission funds, seven councils of government (COGs) and eight senior colleges in eastern

North Carolina were supported during the winter of 1973-1974 to develop strategies and tactics for expanding service-learning opportunities for all eastern North Carolina young people. A major intent of these developmental grants to the colleges and COGs was to raise the awareness of the potential for youth service and the possibilities of educational alternatives in service situations. Immediate impacts are modest, but an NCIO notion is that by raising the questions, getting interested individuals together, and providing data on what is happening in local areas and throughout the country, local area leaders will find an appropriate way to make possible service-learning opportunities for young people.

new directions for NCIO

These student-originated and comprehensive youth involvement programs provide a clue to a transition phase which NCIO has been experiencing since late 1973.

The nagging question, "Why shouldn't there be public service-oriented programs for all fifteen- to twenty-two-year-olds?" and the reports from the 1971 White House Conference on Youth, the John D. Rockefeller III Task Force on Youth, and the booklet "From Adolescence to Adulthood," all suggested that service-learning principles and administrative models might have something to offer most youth service programs.

NCIO has proposed to the educational and governmental leadership in North Carolina that a Youth Involvement Assistance Center be established to work toward the long-range goal of providing at least one three-month service-learning opportunity to all fifteen- to twenty-two-year-olds in the state. NCIO has also proposed that it devote full attention to creating youth-initiated service-learning opportunities. The future role of NCIO is unclear and dependent upon policy decisions of its dual sponsors.

conclusion

The NCIO role as a statewide enabler and support base for fostering youth involvement with public needs can be best evaluated against the following criteria:

- Has NCIO focused on public and human needs as defined by indigenous communities?
- Has there been interinstitutional (community, university, state) cooperation in the project areas?

- Has interagency cooperation among public agencies been facilitated through service-learning programs?
- Has the "level of dialogue" at all levels of involvement been raised so that problem-solving conceptualization and action are improved?
- Has student involvement through service-learning been an effective catalyst for the above?

In short, NCIO has not wanted to be judged on the number of agency placements created for students or the success or failure of isolated projects, but we have been looking toward cooperation among institutions and individuals who are meeting social needs in specialized areas. We have looked toward, in the development of the young, the attitudes and conceptual orientations that will enable them to see beyond current crises and particular projects to the integration of many minds and hands and spirits. We have looked toward the development of servant-leaders who will take the risks, imagine the ideologies, and provide the structures so that "caring for persons, the more able and the less able serving each other" can be seen as a rock upon which a good society is built. In the words of Robert Greenleaf (1972, p. 1), "If a better society is to be built, one that is more just and more loving, one that provides greater creative opportunity for its people, then the most open course is to raise both the capacity to serve and the very performance as servant of existing major institutions by new regenerative forces operating within them." From the limited evidence at hand, service-learning internships expose some of those "regenerative forces" to their personal responsibilities for serving public needs.

The NCIO, as a state approach to providing service-learning opportunities for students, has been a minor catalytic agent for opening up learning environments in the public sector. Its efforts indicate that young people can serve with distinction, sound learning based on individual need does occur, and institutional processes are challenged about how well they give the young responsibility for themselves and the world around them. I don't think NCIO processes are a model, as the SREB report suggests, but I am sure that the service-learning model offers an appropriate response "to the needs of youth for public involvement responsibilities and for educational alternatives in public need settings."

references

Greenleaf, R. "The Institution as Servant." Cambridge: Center for Applied

Studies (17 Dunster St., Cambridge, Mass. 02138), 1972. (See also his "The Servant as Leader" and "Trustees as Servants.")

Hoose, H. "Service-Learning Internships: A Look at the Influences of Service-Learning Internships on 56 Students." Raleigh: North Carolina Internship Office (116 West Jones St., Raleigh, N.C. 27603), 1973.

North Carolina Internship Office. "A Notebook on Service-Learning." Raleigh, 1972.

Southern Regional Education Board. "Service-Learning Internships in North Carolina—A Report on the North Carolina Internship Office." Atlanta (130 Sixth Street Northwest, Atlanta, Georgia 30313), 1973.

Robert Sigmon is director of the North Carolina Internship Office in Raleigh. He has been involved in arranging public need-based learning opportunities in the South since 1964. With the American Friends Service Committee he directed a "Quaker Peace Corps" type program, then joined the Resource Development Internship Project of the Southern Regional Education Board in 1967. He came to North Carolina state government in 1970 to further spread the service-learning style of student involvement.

Students are playing a significant role in expanding the options in field experience education, in pioneering new ways of functioning—independent and self-initiating—and in creating mature relationships with faculty.

role of the student

mary ellen quinn
louise sellars

In the late 1960s and early 1970s college and university students demanded broad changes in what they learned and how they learned it. Some of their criticisms seemed to echo Brownell's censures: that higher education was treated not as life but only as a preparation for life; that the student was placed in a social vacuum, a "recess from life"; and that higher education as almost completely divorced in the student's experience from significant practice (Brownell, 1952). Students clamored for relevance and meaningfulness. Among others, Heist and Wilson (1968) reported that students complained about "the rigidity of the curricula and academic experiences" and the lack of "opportunity to pursue their interests or to learn in ways most advantageous to them." In responding to the demands and needs of the students many colleges and universities began to explore, develop, or expand field education experience, experiences that Mayhew (1971) contends are the right of every student.

types of field experiences

In a 1972 study of undergraduate field experience education at Michigan State University (Quinn, 1972) the following student projects were reported: One student visited and lived in abandoned World War II incarceration camps in California, interviewed former inmates, and compiled his findings and reflections into a book to be published. Another student lived, worked, and studied for two months in a California desert—a scientific research project. A young woman spent a term touring and acting with a West Coast theatre group. A young man lived with and observed the Amish as a means of getting background material for the project he designed. Another young man established, edited, and published a newspaper for a religious organization. And another prepared both radio and television broadcasts for his field study. One student went abroad with a friend where together they gathered data for a comparative study of the teaching techniques of British and American professors. Another student arranged interviews with a group of London businessmen for his self-designed study. One student did research for a senator, another interned in an attorney general's office, and still another spent time working and studying in the Democratic offices in the state capitol building. Experiences included jobs in a CPA firm, in an auditing department, with the Cooperative Service in Washington, in an office on campus, and with the foreign exchange students in another university. Some of the students described field education experiences in probation courts, in the police department, in reform schools, in juvenile homes, and in welfare agencies.

Service-oriented experiences abounded. Some of the students worked with small inner-city businesses as management consultants, planned and set up community recreation programs and centers, interned in day-care centers, and worked with the physically handicapped, the emotionally disturbed, and the mentally retarded.

Other students were involved in cross-cultural experiences, encounter groups, leadership studies, family counseling, summer camps, and neighborhood surveys. One student studied some social problems of the inner city of Detroit; another, the social welfare system in Europe. One investigated the deterioration of housing in a specific area of a city; another worked at the socialization of former mental patients.

Some students participated in field experiences that took them away from campus for two to three hours or days at a time. Other field work lasted two or three weeks or an entire term. Students reported going to the Appalachian Mountains for geological study, to the deep South for a study of the park system, and to the East and South for forestry study. Many of the field experiences were primarily observational in nature with some discussion or presentation by experts or professionals in the field; others were research oriented and actively involved the students in such follow-up projects as map making, soil analysis, or water study. At times these learning periods were preliminary to a more active participation in subsequent field experience education. Although these learning experiences seem to "run the gamut," they parallel much field education of students in other colleges and universities. Reports and surveys point out the growth and development of field experiences, foreign study, service-learning projects, work-study programs, and many off-campus education projects falling under the independent study category.

assumptions about learning

A review of the literature reveals that many educators recognize that some very basic assumptions or theories about learning give support to the concept of field experience education. First, the testing of theory in practical situations adds a most valuable contribution to the learning process. Henderson (1970) claims that "the interweaving of the theoretical and the practical should accelerate learning and make it more lasting. It should result in a higher degree of competence in the individual." The student develops a most important aspect of learning, the ability to place objects and events in new relationships.

When this application of theory directs itself outwardly to the community, to the service of others, or to societal issues, another dimension is approached. Dunivant (1969) points out that the cue words of college students are *relevance, meaningfulness,* and *action.* Measured against these criteria many college courses prove woefully lacking. However, the involvement demanded by field education experiences fulfills the needs implied by these terms. "[The student's] interaction with his environment can be so structured as to enable him to gain awareness and understanding of the world in a conscious, systematic fashion, i.e., to learn; and simultaneously, to render service to this community by helping to meet its needs and solve its problems, i.e., to *serve*" (Dunivant, 1969, p. 2). Sanford (1967) also notes that the situation can be meaningful if students are fully immersed in the realities of a problem situation; that is, engaged with it and concerned with bringing about some desirable changes.

A second assumption of field experience education, one so basic and yet at the same time frequently disregarded, is that each individual is unique and has different needs. Educational programs should reflect the interests and capabilities of different students and should give them opportunities to respond at the time, in the manner, and at the pace best suited to the individual. Many types of field experience education are structured in such a way that these goals may be achieved. However, basic to an environment that allows this type of growth is, according to Heist and Wilson (1968), a teacher-student relationship that is supportive of the student. Students interviewed for this study were quite vocal about this.

Another assumption, supported by research evidence, is that individual development, whether it be a greater sense of responsibility, self-reliance, self-direction, or independence, is fostered by field study experiences. In the Michigan State University study one faculty member stated, "I see the objectives of our program as personality growth, learning to take interpersonal risks, and learning to deal with oneself. The particular content is less important to me than what the person learns about how one deals with life." Similar comments from other faculty working with students involved in field experience education indicate a strong support for the view that the college has a responsibility to help develop the whole personality and to be concerned with other than cognitive goals. Students also saw the importance of such activity and incorporated these values into their own set of objectives. As one student said, "You're given a chance to do your own learning. You're not spoon fed by a professor and expected to regurgitate this data which the professor has thrown on you during the class. You more or less evaluate yourself, think for yourself, and learn for yourself."

This idea that content or the cognitive aspects of the learning situation play a role secondary to that of acquiring attitudes or values was expressed by another faculty member. His hopes were that field experiences would thrust the students so forcefully into reality that they would discover that learning is an ongoing process, something that takes place because they make it take place and that need not be confined to any particular place or time. He said, "The most important thing is to know what learning is all about, to realize learning is not a set of abstract things to be memorized or to be combined. It is to be engaged in ongoing social and natural life and at the same time to be able to pull these things together, to realize that it is a lifelong process that is not just related to formal structural learning situations. You learn the excitement of being able to interpret your own experiences every day in a framework that allows you to both stand off and be involved. It's a whole mind set; if you get the hang of it it gives you a richness of perspective and makes you demand things of yourself."

new student role

Given this understanding of the nature of field experience education, the student obviously has a different role from the one he traditionally has in the classroom, although the role differences are not antithetical. The student has usually been passive. He has been "taught." He has been the receptacle for objective "knowledge." He has been educated and evaluated and he wonders why. At the end of this process of being imbued with information, he finds it very hard to act on the basis of it. Thus, as the object of an educational process, the student's role has not been one of real involvement. There has been little opportunity for posing questions based on real working situations; little opportunity for determining goals, defining potential, for critical awareness as opposed to the superficial recognition that certain things exist. Absent has been the challenge to be conscious of, to take responsibility for, to define and to limit one's own potential.

Field experience education can provide that challenge. But much diversity in practice stems from the nature of this newer student role: the student as subject in the learning experience. The existing models of and experiments in field experience education vary in method and approach. They differ in the amount of freedom and subsequent responsibility afforded and in the degree to which the student is conscious of and participates directly in determining the nature of his experience.

The changing student role requires new definitions—of students, educators, institutions. When students are faced with independence, freedom, and requirements such as self-motivation and self-criticism, then variations develop as relationships evolve, teacher to student to institution, with transformations in the responsibilities demanded of each. There is struggle and trial and error involved. For the student this active self-determining role is not as easy as resting within the security of passivity. But the evolution of a newer, fully conscious, active approach to education in the field, within society as opposed to the confines of the classroom and a course syllabus, is a step forward. It can provide for open engagement in a search for the action-learning-vocation based on ideals, centering learning in living and doing.

As field experience education offers increased responsibility with the independence and freedom to define and limit one's own potential, it demands more of the student. The experiential role requires sensitivity, political and cultural awareness, as well as respect. When learning is dialogical as opposed to narrative, when it is experiential, success depends upon real and meaningful relationships, with advisors, field advisors, resource persons, with everyone from whom we have something to learn. The "do your own thing" attitude prevalent in American culture, and particularly characteristic of independent field study, can be a barrier to this type of education. It can prevent the essential interaction: the objective criticism and sharing that are so basic to a dialogical approach to learning. The tendency to rely too heavily on individual freedom and autonomy can leave the student a dilettante, wandering from experience to experience, from culture to culture, like a tourist indulging in sheer experience for the sake of it, rather than integrating, interpreting, and tying experiences into meaningful themes.

Only in an atmosphere of trust and mutual respect, free of the arrogance implied in "do your own thing" or the exploitation that can result from the "freedom" that is often license, can students and educators work together to define their new roles. The student is challenged in planning the field experiences and determining educational goals. He is required to define those goals and to discover, often through the experience, his own limits. The evaluative process also requires a high degree of sensitivity and respect. The teacher is not to judge autocratically, independent of the student's own perception of his success or failure. At the same time, no one is self-taught and the student must remain open and attuned to an objective, critical appraisal of his experience.

conclusion

Field experience education offers the challenge of self-motivation, the opportunity for self-knowledge and self-determined goals; it begins an active process of centering learning in experience and action in ideals. But it is trying and can be painful. Through this dynamic, in which growth is often found in failure, comes self-discovery. Field experience education presupposes self-knowledge of motives, a careful balance of free action and a sense of where

The Role of the Student

The basic role of the student in field experience education is to become an independent, self-initiating learner, but there are many subcomponents of this role. In accomplishing his task he must fulfill many of the following roles:

Initiator	1. Identifies, seeks, finds, and secures the help and co-operation he needs, often in a context alien to his experience.
Problem Solver & Decision Maker	2. Functions in an open system; he has to define and solve the problems as they arise and make decisions in the course of carrying out his project which affect his and the personal lives of others.
Cultural Analyst & Strategist	3. Understands well enough the cultural context in which he is trying to function to work effectively in it.
Interactor	4. Relates effectively with his faculty supervisor, co-workers, clients or customers; able to stay in touch with them and work through emotionally difficult relationships.
Information Source & Network Developer	5. Develops his own information sources instead of relying on those provided by an instructor.
Free Agent	6. Functions on his own in a support system in which rewards are given for productive work done to develop and carry out workable solutions to particular and often unforeseen problems rather than for predetermined correct answers to set problems, and in an unstructured setting without the classroom support systems of assignments, syllabi, and tests.
Value Clarifier	7. Makes value judgments in arriving at these workable (compromise) solutions or decisions which he would not be expected to make in his classroom work.
Communicator	8. Is able to communicate effectively through the spoken and written word, through listening and reading non-verbal communication, and to be emotionally involved with the people he is learning with and from: he is not allowed to act as if learning were a completely objective activity.
Recipient	9. Is able to receive and utilize criticism constructively.

cultural taboos lie—knowing whether a particular "desire" is instinctive, cultural, personal; a product of thought, contemplation, or the unconscious.

Students have had a very significant historical role in the creation and expansion of field experience education, providing through their active involvement in the struggles for civil rights, peace, and educational reform in the late sixties and early seventies the impetus for this development. The nature of this type of education requires a new definition of roles for all of the principal participants, especially that of the student.

references

Brownell, B. *The College and the Community*. New York: Harper, 1952.

Dunivant, N., Jr. *Bridging the Gap*. Winston-Salem, N.C.: The Winston-Salem Service-Learning Project in Community Resource Development, 1969.

Heist, P., and Wilson, R. "Curricular Experiences for the Creative." In P. Heist (Ed.), *The Creative College Student: An Unmet Challenge*. San Francisco: Jossey-Bass, 1968.

Henderson, A. D. *The Innovative Spirit*. San Francisco: Jossey-Bass, 1970.

Mayhew, L. N., and Ford, P. J. *Changing the Curriculum*. San Francisco: Jossey-Bass, 1971.

Quinn, M. E. "An Investigation of Undergraduate Field Study Experiences at Michigan State University." Unpublished doctoral dissertation, Michigan State University, East Lansing, 1972.

Sanford, N. *Where Colleges Fail*. San Francisco: Jossey-Bass, 1967.

Mary Ellen Quinn is currently serving as provincial administrator for the Omaha Province of the Sisters of Mercy. She was dean and then academic vice president at the College of St. Mary in Omaha, Nebraska, from 1964 until 1973. From 1970 to 1972 she was released for doctoral studies at Michigan State University where she studied off-campus learning experiences and developed guidelines for colleges and universities initiating field study programs. Louise Sellars is a 1974 graduate of Friends World College, having completed a field study project in Kenya as her final project. She worked as part of the staff of the Friends World College Learning Center in Machakos, Kenya.

The role of the faculty supervisor is extremely complex, and so loosely defined that he often does little real supervising.

the faculty supervisor

tyrone r. baines

It is the intent of this paper to vigorously support the use of field experiences as learning devices and as an alternative method of teaching and to look at the various actors in the process, focusing on the uses and misuses of the faculty supervisor. It will prescribe what the role of an effective faculty supervisor should be. The discussion is based on my experience as a social work intern and a government intern, as agency supervisor of a government internship program, and as the faculty supervisor and internship program administrator of a university program.

three models

In order to understand the supervisor's role we must examine the three primary models for field experiences. The first, the medical school model, is one of the oldest and most accepted. It is based on the recognition that in addition to "knowing about" people doctors must "know how" to treat people. In this framework, the student spends the first year or two in the traditional manner, "learning about." He often takes a trip to observe the organization, hospital, or clinic where he is likely to perform his skills. During the next year, he goes to the hospital and begins treating patients under the supervision of a licensed doctor. This supervision tapers off and the medical student is ready to spend his first year in the medical organization as a resident. This model has been adopted by other professions such as social work.

Like the first, the second model recognizes that there is a gap between theory and reality in all professions and the best way to prepare competent students is to reduce that gap during the student's education process. A major difference between this model and the first is that the internship is mandatory in the latter and highly desirable in the former. In this model, the student spends the first year or two studying on the college campus. Then an attempt is made to find the student a position in some agency, preferably one related to his discipline. He may work for a summer, a few months during the school year, a semester of the school year, or a few hours a day after classes. This widely used model assumes that the experience acquired makes the student a better employee after his field work is over. But it has been severely criticized for being unstructured, haphazard, ineffective as a means of ensuring learning, and a tool for the misuse of student labor. This model has been used by many disciplines, political science, sociology, law, biology, chemistry, public administration, business, and many others.

The third model, which is the most current, combines elements of the first two and adds more structure to the field experience process. This model recognizes that most of the "doing" professions require an internship; that the bridge between theory and reality must be built. As an additional method of teaching, the field experience must have as much structure as any other teaching method. The third model insists that a typical internship is "a 10-15 week, full-time assignment in which work and learning tasks are clearly defined, academic credit is awarded, and some stipend is available" (Kiel and Sigmon, 1973, p. 8). This model was clearly a reaction to the criticisms raised about the second one. Therefore, it is being used by the same disciplines which used the previous model.

Although field experiences have different forms and structures, they should primarily have one purpose: to promote learning. A work experience that does not contain learning cannot be called an educational device. Institutions of higher education are committed to learning and must not support programs which take the student off the campus under the guise that merely being away from school teaches them something. As the university's representative, the faculty supervisor must ensure that the field experience does provide an opportunity for learning and that the student has access to it.

supervision vs. administration

In many cases, the faculty supervisor is also the program administrator. These two roles may be incompatible, demanding different skills. Supervision is a specific process that requires the individual to have an in-depth knowledge of the student and the subject matter he is expected to learn. The faculty supervisor must maintain close contact with both the student and the agency supervisor. And he must abandon his traditional role of offering a general opportunity to learn in order to provide each student with the specific opportunity to learn. This shift is very demanding and time consuming (see Schmidt, 1973).

On the other hand, the program administrator has the function of making sure that all the actors in the field experience process are working together toward a common goal. He needs broad expertise in planning, coordinating, and developing rather than specific sensitivity to the problems of individual students. For one individual to handle these two roles is a very difficult task in any university setting, especially if the university has a substantial number of students in field experiences. However, since many schools do combine these two functions, the faculty supervisor will be discussed here as the person who has these combined functions.

functions

In general terms, the faculty supervisor is responsible for running the university program. The scope of his job depends on the university's commitment to the program, his own commitment, the amount of release time provided him, and the availability of host agencies for placement. More specifically, faculty advisors may perform all the following functions:

1. Designing the field experience program.
2. Securing university approval of the program.
3. Selecting and supervising the students.
4. Establishing host agencies and maintaining relations with them.
5. Acting as troubleshooter between the university, the host agency, the student, and the agency supervisor.
6. Reporting on the outcome of field learning experience (evaluations, grades, and reports).

Field experience can be the most valuable part of a student's education or it can be one of the major cop-outs. Some positions are expertly designed and are producing the desired results, students who are well prepared for their chosen careers. Others are not worth the paper on which they are written. The faculty supervisor is a major factor in determining which of these outcomes occurs.

Design. Although there is no one best design for field experience, it must, as I emphasized earlier, ensure that learning takes place. An effective design has the following elements: (1) clearly defined goals for each student which manifest themselves in terms of a concrete project, (2) continuous supervision and monitoring of the field experience, and (3) a concrete tool and procedure for evaluation. The absence of these three components is the major shortcoming of much field experience education. Making sure they are present is primarily the supervisor's responsibility, since he is ultimately the one responsible for demonstrating that field experiences are providing learning.

Academic Credit. Another aspect of the faculty advisor's job is to secure academic credit for the field experience. Students, universities, faculty members, and host agencies are more committed to programs which receive credit. The design of the program must be adapted accordingly. When the supervisor is trying to get credit for field experience he should develop a proposal that includes clear goals, close academic supervision, specific projects and definite evaluative tools. As a member of the academic community he should be aware of its goals and should use all his sensitivity in writing and presenting the proposal for academic approval. Field experience needs to be presented, not as something revolutionary, but as another means of producing the best educated student possible.

Selecting and Supervising Students. Besides the academic record, financial need, sex, and race are often selection criteria because agencies are more likely to accept women and minority group members. Financial need is frequently considered because many field experiences are remunerative. However, these qualifications are often outweighed by such considerations as student interest, motivation, maturity, and ability to get along with people. Field experience programs must keep in mind that one type of student will do well in one setting and will do poorly in another. Since students and field experiences differ, a great deal of attention must be given to attempting to match the student with the host agency or extra-university setting. Selection is crucial to program continuity because agencies do not like to accept poor students and may not accept students from a university on a continuing basis if they are not chosen with care.

The other dimension of selecting students is supervising them. The degree of supervision will vary from student to student, but the faculty advisor must be accessible to each student on an ongoing basis. He should have enough expertise in the experience area to guide the student in his learning process. The status of being a student means identifying with an academic institution. The faculty advisor should take advantage of this natural tendency and use it as a means of helping the student find connections between the academic world and the real world.

Agency Relations. The various actors in the field experience should be depicted as partners in learning. The faculty supervisor must develop this partnership and help to maintain it. There is no substitute for a host agency which values the mutual benefits for the university, the student, and the agency. Many subtle benefits, such as an opportunity for agency personnel to learn supervision, are frequently overlooked. The faculty supervisor should guide the agency supervisor in dealing with students, for they are not regular employees. Maintaining relations with the host agency is both a formal and informal process. The informal process is often more important than the formal. The faculty supervisor should stop by the agency during pleasant times as well as stressful times. The relationship between the faculty and agency supervisors can facilitate the student's experience with the agency. There must be an atmosphere of openness and trust between these individuals. They must not compete for ownership of the student. They must trust that each is competent in his area, yet ensure that each is giving his best to the student. This function is very time consuming but is very important.

The determination of whether interns should be paid and who should pay them is an aspect of the relationship between the faculty supervisor and the host agency. The paying of interns symbolizes the agency's commitment to their value and helps ensure that the agency will take the experience seriously. If the student is not in an agency, there should still be some source of funding. The pay helps defray the special costs of internships, such as transportation and noncampus attire. These are realistic expenses which must be handled. Many agencies feel that the mere fact that they are making their facilities and personnel available to the student is pay enough. The faculty supervisor can help define reasons why students should be paid and make sure that students do in fact produce the benefits which have been defined. But the most convincing argument for paying students is their productivity. The faculty supervisor can only be a facilitator in this area.

Evaluation. Faculty supervisors should take the initiative in evaluation. The assessment should seek wide participation by faculty members, student, and agency staff. There is no one best method of evaluating field experience. Many of the traditional tools such as examinations, demonstrations, and writing can be used. The device is not important as long as it is consistent with the goals of the experience and accurately indicates the objectives which have been established. From the student's point of view, the experience should result in some knowledge and skills which could not have been acquired from textbooks in the classroom and a grade which will help him achieve his ultimate goal, the degree. The university and the agency may have other goals, such as curriculum innovation or agency-university cooperation. Whatever the goals of the various actors are, it is very important that creative and different approaches such as field experience education document their outcomes to reduce criticism of their validity.

In sum, the wide variety of field experiences suggests that the faculty supervisor should not also be the program administrator. The supervisory role requires different skills from that of the program administrator. The administrator should coordinate all the institution's internship programs and handle administrative matters such as acquiring credit for internships and establishing contact with host agencies at the institutional level. The separation of these roles should free the faculty supervisor to concentrate on supervision.

references

Kiel, D. H., and Sigmon, R. L. "Toward Multi-Dimensional Internship Programs in State and Local Government." Raleigh, N.C.: North Carolina Internship Office, 1973.

Schmidt, D. M. "Supervision: A Sharing Process." *Child Welfare,* 1973, 7, 436-446.

Tyrone R. Baines is associate professor of political science and director of the Public Administration Program at North Carolina Central University, Durham. He is also director of the Public Administration Internship Program. Formerly he directed the Office of Economic Opportunity Internship Program, Washington, D.C.

Supervisors use the discipline of labor, with its demand for action and usefulness, to motivate progress toward educational and manpower goals.

role of the agency supervisor

william r. ramsay

A few years ago, a law student completing his final report on an internship project in the area of legal services remarked to his agency supervisor, "You know, the way I write this report will not just make a difference between an A and a B in a course, it will make a difference in the lives of people." This student was standing on the bridge between academic studies and the world of reality. Assisting him in crossing this bridge and seeing the view from its span was an agency supervisor. Supervisors of students in field experience situations are special kinds of educators. Typically, they are professionals in their fields and have other supervisory responsibilities.

This discussion is limited to specific opportunities for and methods of supervising students, rather than supervisory techniques in general. Certainly, basic tenets of good supervision apply to the use of students in work situations as well as to regular employees. Different objectives, however, and differences between students and nonstudents require special approaches in supervising field experience. This paper examines the characteristics of student workers; the types of structures for supervising student field experience are noted; supervisory functions are suggested; and the potentials of good supervision are summarized.

It is assumed for purposes of this discussion that productive work is a factor in the field experience situation. The amount of productive work will vary according to the structure used and the objectives of the particular program; however, implicit in a discussion of supervision is the expectation of some product or service. The characteristics of students, therefore, are discussed in terms of the possibilities and limitations of students as manpower, an assumption which should be recognized by a supervisor both for effective manpower utilization and for greatest learning.

characteristics of students

One rather obvious quality of student manpower is its short-term availability. Internships or other field experience situations generally range from one month to one year. This time factor has important implications for planning effective programs. The tasks assigned must be possible to accomplish within the time limits of the arrangement. A schedule of progress must be concentrated in a much shorter period than would normally be the case with other employment. Furthermore, the student's short-term involvement and perception of time in general is important in terms of his own expectations and attitudes. What seems like a short time to a supervisor relative to other forms of employment seems often like a long time to the student who is used to thinking in much smaller increments of time. One of the problems resulting from these different perceptions is related to expected results. Students tend to think they can accomplish more in a short time than they can. Supervisors may err on the other side, thinking they can perform less than they can. If students are encouraged in unrealistic expectations of accomplishment, their experience will end in frustration. On the other hand, if not enough expectation is built into the program, an opportunity for stretching the student to apply his utmost resources may have been lost.

Another characteristic of student manpower is its orientation toward impact. Students desire a personal involvement and are very much concerned with being able to "make a difference." This desire for impact is a powerful motivating force and can be used by good supervision in place of the traditional motivating tools of salary, promise of advancement, benefits, and position. Students are concerned with compensation or other forms of support, but these are not major factors as they will be when the students as graduates are considering regular employment. It is therefore especially important for supervisors to encourage personal involvement and to help associate student efforts with results. Realistic goals against which achievement can be measured can be very helpful in meeting the student's need to see the results of effort. Interpretation is also essential to help the student see the relationships between his effort and the efforts of others toward longer range goals of the agency or program.

An attitude often found among students, perhaps reflecting their orientation toward impact, is the feeling that "no one will really listen to me." Experience with many student work situations indicates that this is not nearly so often the case in reality as it is in the image of the student. A student is apt to think no one will listen so he doesn't speak, or when he encounters first difficulties in suggesting what he considers new ideas he retreats with the defense that he knew no one would listen. Progress is most often extremely hard work and those who are in the action part of the world know that many constructive ideas die not because they are poor ideas, but because there is no program for implementing them. It is relatively easy to decry what is wrong with a situation or even to say what should be done. It is much harder to get on with the task of improving it. This issue of assumed or real barriers presents special problems with student workers, since their commitment is toward short-range objectives and they want a personal involvement in results.

Another characteristic of student workers is their relative freedom. Partly because they are involved for short periods of time they are free from the responsibilities of longer range interest. They can be used for short-term projects in many cases more effectively than can longer term employees because they can devote full time and attention to one task. Students are able to function at a great variety of levels in an organization and do not need to be restricted to the usual hierarchies of an organization chart. One supervisor observed that his students served as a form of media, carrying information from various levels of the organization to other levels, in a way which other forms of communication could not accomplish. Students are not restrained by experience. Lack of experience limits what they can do, but also provides an opportunity for a fresh look and a new approach. As one student expressed, "I haven't learned yet what can't be done." Students are expendable. They can afford to make mistakes and therefore to take risks that persons with longer term employment could not or would not. Because they are students they are excused for mistakes and the results can be handled with a minimum of disruption. Recognition of this opens up a wider vista for potential assignments and may take students into areas that can be better served by this form of manpower than by any other.

Another important characteristic of good field experience programs is that the student has educational goals as well as manpower goals. This dual purpose can add important dimensions to the student's manpower usefulness and affects supervision. Because of educational goals he tends to undertake his tasks with a questioning attitude rather than simply carrying out instructions. This approach can be considered a nuisance but also can be vital to certain types of assignments. Students may bring to their work situation a greater inquisitiveness and desire for understanding than is often present in other workers. Students are concerned with meaning and have a broad interest in the implications of actions and programs. Students also represent potential channels for inputs of information, technical assistance, and other resources of the university or college with which they are associated. These can be used by a supervisor in enhancing productivity and learning. All of these characteristics will not apply to all situations, but a recognition of the special circumstances of student manpower is important to effective manpower achievement and the related educational development of the student.

structures

A variety of structural patterns for field experience is possible. Several of these are mentioned briefly here to indicate some of the different supervisory situations which result. Perhaps the most often used off-campus experience structure is simply the traditional position in an organization. The student is "hired" as an employee and shows up on an organization chart as an intern, assistant, or some other such term. Supervision of students in such positions follows traditional methods, using job descriptions, office procedures, and the usual set of relationships with other employees. Berea College uses its 1400 students as its basic source of manpower and every college department, academic and otherwise, is also a student labor department utilizing students. Students work and learn in a great variety of assignments from typing to computer programming and from weaving to teaching adult literacy. Most colleges have some employment programs for students but few are designed and supervised as field experience.

In a second type of structure the student might be termed an "honored guest." In these cases he is generally in a nonproducing situation where his main functions are to observe and prepare academic reports. Supervision in these cases is generally limited to arranging schedules for orientation and seeing that these are followed and that some information and understanding is in fact passed on.

Another internship structure gives the student the role of special assistant. He holds a position, but generally it is outside the usual personnel structures. A student may be an assistant to a city manager for a period or an aide to a legislator. Generally he receives highly personal supervision, and the main benefit derived is his association with a professional of high caliber. If care is not taken in this situation the student may end up being an errand boy doing tasks that arise from day to day with little planning or progress toward objectives.

A project is the basis of a fourth structure. In this case the student is given a task with specific objectives which can be accomplished within his time period. Supervision in the form of planning and direction is called for early in the stages of such an approach and then the student often proceeds on his own initiative with little close direction. A reporting system is important here, and some guidance is needed to see that time is not wasted and objectives are being met. In the most effective project arrangements the student becomes largely self-supervised within the structure established.

Any one of these or other structures may be used effectively, depending on the particular situation of the agency involved and the educational relationships. In general, the project approach is considered superior in terms of actual accomplishment and learning and it requires less day to day supervision than the position approach. Careful planning is especially important. An example of this approach was used by the Training & Technology Project (TAT) of Oak Ridge Associated Universities. With the assistance of the universities a group of students were selected and assigned to seek out and collect information on graduates of the manpower training program of TAT. Students were trained in interview techniques and given assistance in locating graduates. They were dispatched to the points in the country where most graduates had found employment. Using a predeveloped system of forms they collected information and sent them in to the central office. At the same time each student pursued a related study project of his own on which he was required to report at the end of the period. In three months' time the students were able to collect a significant amount of data for an effective report on the status of graduates of this training program. In addition they prepared reports on their own individual studies and had seminars with university faculty assigned to each area. The nature of the supervision was different from that normally found in a typical supervisor-employee relationship. Once started the initiative passed largely to the student rather than being retained by the supervisor.

supervisor's dual role

Regardless of the structure used, the agency supervisor has a double role in relation to students engaged in field experience. He must see the student as both worker and learner. His special contribution to the student's development is in helping the student relate through his work to the real world. This means holding the student to productive endeavor even when it is difficult and even when the results are imperfect. Supervisors know that they must deal with imperfect situations. They must often make decisions with lack of full information and choose among undesirable alternatives. Action is unavoidable and work must be tested against the criterion of usefulness, not simply satisfying an academic requirement. This special discipline is part of labor. The teaching function of the supervisor is primarily to interpret. The ability to relate actual individual experience to the experience of others and to models, theories, and information learned in the classroom does not develop automatically. The supervisor plays a critical role in helping the student bridge the distance between the world of action and the world of reflection. In general, supervisors are responsible for some output in terms of product or service. They must see that the objectives of the organization are met and that the labor under their supervision is directed toward that end. However, the student laborer is an end in himself and success is measured in part by his development. The supervisor must, therefore, integrate the educational needs of the student and the production needs of the task for effective learning and service.

steps in supervision

Absolutely basic to all good field experience situations is effective *planning.* The position, project, or other form of assignment should be carefully defined and all parties should have a clear understanding about what is expected in terms of both productivity and educational growth. The supervisor's job is to apply his knowledge of what is possible, given time constraints, resources, and his organization's purpose and scope. It is useful to define the intern's assignment in general terms and then in very specific terms with indications of steps to be taken, at least in its beginning stages. At the same time, it is important to keep from putting too tight a lid on the project or position before a student is involved himself.

Next, the supervisor should participate in the *recruitment* and *selection* of the students with whom he will be working. At a minimum he should describe the qualifications necessary and in the optimum situation he would actually conduct interviews and help make the final selection. Many internships or field experience situations founder on the rocks of different perceptions of what is expected. This possibility can most effectively be cleared up by face to face contact between the agency supervisor, the academic representative, and the prospective student. Supervisory involvement in the selection process can also emphasize concern with standards. A professional personnel approach toward selecting the student lets him know that he is considered important and is expected to meet standards, and that he will play an important role in the organization.

Once an internship is planned and a prospective student identified the supervisor must see that the necessary *supporting structures* are provided. Space will be needed, contacts with other personnel, materials and supplies, equipment and basic information on how to get things done. This support structure is essential for the intern or student to function quickly and effectively.

An *orientation* by the supervisor which gives the student information on resources and on the system in which he is to accomplish his objectives is essential. It is important for the student to be oriented first to his specific work situation at the beginning of his program. The immediate questions of Where do I fit? How do I get things done? What is expected of me here? have first priority. Often the more general orientation relating the particular experience to the general goals of the field experience program is better accomplished after the student is somewhat secure in his field experience situation. If this broad approach is attempted in detail before placement it may seem to the student to be an academic exercise. But when the student is functioning and well grounded in his agency, it takes on real meaning and can be very helpful. The most important part of the agency orientation is an understanding of the objectives of the assignment and of the setting in which they are to be reached.

It is also important at the very beginning to establish a *schedule.* This should be done with the student and should include reporting periods, time for consultation, dates for initial steps to be taken, and at least the indication of likely deadlines for different stages. The schedule may be revised from time to time, but no good project should begin without a preliminary schedule.

During the student's assignment, *guidance and direction* is important, both at regularly scheduled periods and between times. Through this supervisory attention to the student's progress standards of performance should be stressed and the production of the work assigned should be measured. It is important to remind the student that what he is doing is important and is to be measured on the basis of usefulness as well as in terms of his own growth. Periodically, in addition to day to day guidance, time should be set aside for a review of progress to date and for schedule revisions. Most effectively, such review should include representatives of the academic institution involved, and perhaps other people within the agency. A system of written reports also is important to direction, review, and the pursuit of objectives.

Interpretation. Throughout the assignment the supervisor should help the student interpret the experience he is having and the relationship between what he is doing and the work of the agency and of others. He should cooperate with the academic institution's representatives in interpreting the student's experience in relation to broader concerns, academic studies, models and theories. Through interaction with the student and his academic representative all parties can grow by learning from each other. Supervisor and student should relate as seekers of knowledge and workers toward common goals, each of whom has particular contributions to make, rather than as master and apprentice, a relationship in which all learning is presumed to flow in one direction. In many cases where the student is assigned a specific project he quickly becomes the expert in his assignment and knows more about the particular situation than either his supervisor or his academic representative. This position can be very stimulating to the student and if supervisors are not threatened the student's "expertise" can be very helpful to the organization.

The supervisor should be sensitive to problems that may develop either in pursuit of the assignment or in the personal relations in which the intern or student is engaged. Most often failure in a field experience situation relates not to the job assignment but to relationships between people. A student should understand in the beginning the policies and standards of the organization and his responsibility of working in this environment. He should be given status and the necessary contacts and tools to do his task. If in spite of this preparation problems develop to the point of impairing the effectiveness of the project or the well-being of the organization or student, termination should probably occur. The machinery for termination should be well established before the program begins and described in the orientation of the student. Close cooperation is necessary in such cases between the supervisor and the academic representative. Failure in an assignment may not mean failure in learning. Sometimes one learns most from negative experience.

Completion and Evaluation. Toward the end of an assignment the supervisory role generally becomes more intense. Considerable assistance should be provided to the student to see that he completes his assigned activity within the time allotted and that he recognizes the necessity of drawing his activities to a close rather than running up to the last minute and suddenly having to leave without having completed anything. A student who really gets interested in his task often has this problem of stopping productivity. An evaluation of the program should be made with the student, before he is gone, in terms of his progress individually and his contribution to the agency. The objectives of this evaluation should be to assist the student in his growth, to improve the field experience program and to help the agency and supervisor in their use of students. After the student leaves, a further evaluation of his contribution and growth is often helpful as a more objective review tempered by time.

modeling

Often the interpersonal relations that develop between a supervisor and a student are among the most significant parts of the student's experience. Taking an interest in the student and his total activities and sharing with him feelings and interests beyond the work situation can be very helpful, particularly where the student is in a new environment. The supervisor, whether or not he wishes such a role, becomes part of the student's image of what it means to be a professional in the world of work. The supervisor is a model which the student may seek to emulate or to reject. This function places a special responsibility on those who supervise student programs to conduct themselves in ways which they would wish others to follow. A willingness to share oneself in this way can make a real difference in the kind of experience a student has and in his views of his profession and his future service.

The supervisor's task includes maintaining effective interaction with the representatives of the educational institution involved. Contacts should be maintained from the early planning stages through the assignment period and beyond for evaluation and follow-up. The relationships can be stimulating and very productive, both for the supervisor in his role in the agency and the academic representative in his role in the university.

summary

Good supervision in a field experience program can assure that everybody gains. An effective program benefits the agency by the contributions of the student; the educational institution benefits by finding a stimulating relationship between the world of reflection and the world of action; and most important, the student benefits by having made a contribution, by learning how to accomplish a task, and by applying his interpretation of his experience to his own understanding and growth. The supervisor uses the discipline of labor with its demand for action and usefulness to motivate, to direct, and to measure progress toward both educational and manpower goals.

William R. Ramsay has been dean of labor at Berea College since 1970. Formerly he directed the Resource Development Program of the Southern Regional Educational Board and served with Oak Ridge Associated Universities from 1955 to 1967. In addition to his responsibilities as labor dean he presently coordinates the activities of the Work-Study Development Project at Berea.

While experiential learning has become a viable educational concept, administrative problems persist in efforts to build it into the structure of a university or college.

institutionalizing experiential learning in a state university

robert f. sexton
john b. stephenson

Not yet a year ago, the University of Kentucky created an Office for Experiential Education to develop and coordinate the off-campus learning activities of all university students. Because of contemporary interest in experiential education we have been asked many times to explain the causes and implications of this development: in essence, to explain how a traditional land grant university instituted a nontraditional program and what the phenomenon means.

Reflection on the development of experiential education at the University of Kentucky leads to two basic questions. The first involves the circumstances surrounding the creation of the Office for Experiential Education at the University of Kentucky. What allowed it to happen, especially in a species of institution whose rigidity and inertia are legendary? The second question concerns the real progress we have made, and what the creation of an administrative office has actually meant in terms of the "institutionalization" of this change.

The first question can be approached through a straightforward narration of events between 1970 and 1973, when the Office was created. It would be additionally helpful if we could abstract from the story of what happened some guiding concepts and principles to explain what happened. If such concepts and principles are valid, they might be put to use again, at the University of Kentucky and elsewhere. Therefore, let us first generalize a bit. For what happened at UK underscores the importance of the following principles, which are no news to social scientists, students of change, or practiced administrators:

1. The use of influentials and elites is essential in the diffusion and adoption of innovations.

2. Timing is important in effecting change, from the standpoint of "client" readiness, competing demands for resources, and support from elites, to name only three aspects.

3. The management and coordination of communications to maintain a proper flow of information is another essential. Communications management is best achieved from points of organizational or system centrality.

4. Innovations should be defined by potential adopters as consistent with existing norms and shared objectives and likely to fulfill felt needs.

5. Of overriding importance is the very basic principle that success in bringing about change is always a mixture of calculated strategy and dumb luck. The mixture may contain 5 percent of the former and 95 percent of the latter!

background events

Leaving these generalities and moving on to the particular experience of the University of Kentucky, our success with experiential education has been the result of a combination of circumstances: some carefully planned over the past four years, some the result of specific institutional characteristics, and some the result of historical accident. To analyze these circumstances, we should examine the role of the Office of the Dean of Undergraduate Studies; the impact of the University Year for Action program; and the importance of a relatively small group of advocates scattered throughout the university.

Dean of Undergraduate Studies. Recognizing the impact on undergraduate programs of a greatly increased emphasis on graduate training in the early and middle sixties, the University of Kentucky attempted to check this swing partly through creating the Office of the Dean of Undergraduate Studies. The position was created in 1967, and was first filled in 1970. In some respects the counterpart of the graduate dean, the undergraduate dean was to improve program effectiveness, improve instruction and advising, and generally attend to those academic concerns which were of common interest to the dozen or so colleges offering undergraduate degrees. The position was filled partly to respond to growing student demands for changes in undergraduate programs, and it quickly became one of the university's more visible symbols of "innovation."

University Year for Action. Through the auspices of the dean of undergraduate studies the university applied for a University Year for Action planning grant in fall, 1971. Following a strategy laid jointly by the dean, a development official with the University Research Foundation, and the director of the Center for Developmental Change (an interdisciplinary campus center which had been important in developing proposals in such areas as welfare research, Peace Corps training, and Appalachian research), the so-called Committee of Forty was assembled to assist in drafting the proposal. The Committee of Forty was large, representative, supportive, and hardworking. For such a sizable and diverse group, it was surprisingly flexible. The planning director, together with the Committee of Forty, organized and submitted a proposal which became the model proposal for UYA in Washington for months—a fact which was later almost our undoing in Lexington.

Washington approved the UYA program proposal, and the university was in the experiential education business on a multicollege basis on January 17, 1972, less than four months after it had first conceived the possibility. Among the institutional changes necessary for getting the grant was the commitment to granting thirty hours of academic credit to students serving in the off-campus program. (Some were incredulous, having already decided that the institution was congenitally incapable of rapid change.)

Of course, scattered but significant off-campus learning activities already existed. In addition to programs in education, social work, and the medical fields, the department of political science had been active in developing state government internship programs which carried fifteen hours of academic credit. These internships had been widely publicized and their patron faculty member was a highly respected scholar. In one respect, then, education through field placements was not a radical innovation at the University of Kentucky.

But the "take-off" for development of experiential learning from such scattered beginnings to the eventual creation of a universitywide Office for Experiential Education depended not only on carefully laid strategies, but on several fortuitous events and decisions.

Academic Credit. One of these was early resolution of the "credit problem" by two members of the Committee of Forty, the vice president for academic affairs and the chairman of the Senate Council. Their plan was to obtain top-level approval for a new universitywide course granting up to fifteen credit hours per semester, but to make its use by any given student contingent on the approval of a department and a college. (The alternative would have been to wait for the unlikely common initiative of around ninety departments to come up with such a course.) This course, University Year for Action 396, will this year be modified as a departmental 300-level course in a gradual, planned move toward an established, universitywide, variable-credit experiential education course.

Locating the Program. Another strategic decision was to place the UYA program under the dean of undergraduate studies, who in turn reports to the vice president for academic affairs. This meant that from the beginning the program benefitted, to a certain degree, from an aura of established academic credibility. This factor became of more crucial importance in later stages than at the beginning. Numerous UYA programs across the nation were initially attached to student services, volunteer offices, or specific professional colleges such as social work or urban studies. To become "institutionalized," these programs must cross the bridge to the academic administration of the institution or expand to engage the broader university community. They are attempting to do this as their federal funding ends, so not only have they lost the initial financial advantage, but they are tackling an academic-political objective which is inherently difficult.

Core Group. Another fortuitous effect of UYA was the establishment of a core of persons on and off the campus, often from unexpected quarters, who could intelligently discuss and rationally visualize the potential of the UYA model. Among these were the vice president for academic affairs, whose support was vital to the effort. Another was a former chairman of the psychology department, a highly respected member of the university community and a person who had had experience as an evaluator of the Peace Corps. This person eventually played an important role in evaluating UYA and later became academic co-director of UYA. Another was the planning director, a vigorous, imaginative assistant professor who subsequently became assistant dean of the College of Arts and Sciences. And almost by accident, one of the authors of this narrative became involved as a member of the Committee of Forty in his role as director of the State Internship Program in Frankfort. Other members of this core group came from such diverse areas as law, architecture, dentistry, community medicine, and vocational education.

outcome

Almost any way one looks at it, the early experience of the UK-UYA program was a near disaster. If there was little time available for planning, there was even less available for implementation. Staffing was completed virtually overnight. There was insufficient time to orient the staff to the complex philosophy of a new program which was to satisfy Washington that poverty was being attacked in a respectable academic fashion, to persuade faculty that learning was taking place under the banner of service, and to convince students that learning objectives could be achieved outside the classroom. Needless to say, the motives of those who participated in those early months were varied and conflicting. The conflict erupted. Surprisingly, it was not faculty who contested an academic ripoff; it was students who contested what they considered another ripoff of the poor. In addition, some agencies felt they had been seriously misled by an overzealous recruiter. Had it not been for a steadfast, mature director who kept a cool head throughout this period of travail, the university would have terminated the project within three months of its beginning.

But UYA survived its nervous launching, which is not to say that it was an unmitigated success even a year or so later. It still faced problems such as its narrow focus on poverty, its requirement of full academic credit for twelve months' full-time work for undergraduates, its apparent inflation of grades, its low rate of faculty involvement in supervision and evaluation, and its exploitation by students with questionable motivation, to name the most important. Nevertheless, UYA has served and is serving its purpose: to allow experimentation with experiential learning just so such problems could be identified and dealt with. And UYA has been a foundation, however shaky it may seem, upon which to build a more solid educational structure.

Thus, the university's experiment with UYA, although not

completely successful, provided both the stimulant and the vehicle for the development of the broader concept of experiential education.

success factors

Several outcomes of the UYA experience, as well as other circumstances only partially related to the program, contributed to whatever success we now enjoy. At the top of this list of circumstances contributing to the maintenance of innovation was the basic credibility of experiential education proponents. In addition to the former chairman of psychology, these included the chairman of the political science department, highly respected faculty in anthropology and sociology, and the deans of the Colleges of Education, Social Professions, and Agriculture, and the vice president for academic affairs. Whatever their individual reasons for supporting the reform, these persons played quiet but decisive roles. Of crucial importance also was the breadth of the small support group—it silenced from the beginning the argument that such education was only advantageous to a small segment of the University or only to the professional colleges. We also saw that a small nuclei of strong supporters, located in the right places and mobilized by the Office of Undergraduate Studies, was as effective as larger numbers would have been.

Another contributing factor was the absence of organized opposition to experiential learning. In part this was due to the role of the persons above, but even more it was the result of the nonthreatening nature of the experiment and pure good luck. The internal proposal which created the Office for Experiential Education had argued not that some radical alternative to tradition was being undertaken, but instead that experiential education should build upon existing programs. The proposal was also reviewed by the deans of all fifteen colleges and many department chairmen, forestalling organized opposition.

Perhaps there was more of a threat to existing experiential programs—but once more the cautious wording of the mandate was important. In other words, assurances were given that existing programs, such as those in education, would not be challenged by a development and coordination office.

Basically, the UYA experience itself made a mixed contribution to the furtherance of experiential education. On the one hand the program had demonstrated the weaknesses of innovation. There were problems with vague or absent criteria for measurement and absence of faculty control of students. The "academic" validity of some of the placements was a constant question as was the fact that many UYA students entered the program with fairly weak academic records. Fortunately, however, these problems were discussed openly if not widely throughout the program and supporters of the concept in general continued to think positively; they felt that inadequacies surfacing in UYA pointed to concerns to be corrected or modified, and not toward elimination. And, in effect, the UYA program really affected only a small group of people. The credit mechanism, although it offered up to thirty hours of undergraduate credit, was couched in safeguards (it was pass/fail in most cases and needed departmental approval to count toward the major) and had been approved only on an experimental basis, so it too posed a limited threat.

In sum, the UYA program's primary contribution to later developments was as a stimulant, not as a paragon of academic virtue. The process of getting the grant stimulated discussion, in a "low-risk" environment, of the advisability of granting large amounts of credit for experience. Administrators and faculty were encouraged during the program's duration to discuss experiential education, and the UYA project staff and advisory committee formed a focal point for this discussion. Students were also exposed to off-campus work in large doses for the first time, and the novelty of their placements resulted in more publicity in the campus media than had been the case with other programs. The availability of federal funds to underwrite a broader office was, of course, a constant advantage in working with the administration.

A major link between UYA and the Office for Experiential Education was the Harris report and recommendation.* Based on interviews with virtually all academic deans, the report showed considerable support for the concept of a centrally coordinated office which would concern itself with the development of off-campus learning experiences. The degree of support shown in this report and its unimpeachable source made it difficult for the vice president and the president to deny support for the new Office for Experiential Education from general fund sources. In July 1973 the new office was created.

*Jesse G. Harris, Jr., "A University Plan for Experiential Education," 1973. Dr. Harris' proposal outlined the process of establishing and the functions of the Office for Experiential Education.

office for experiential education

We now come to the question of how far toward the institutionalization of experiential learning we have come. To begin, let's review briefly the role of the Office for Experiential Education. The office's primary purposes are to coordinate already existing field experience programs (this does not mean, by the way, granting approval for a college or department to place students in an internship), to create a general climate receptive to experiential learning among students and faculty, to develop new field learning opportunities, to facilitate research on the subject, and to disseminate information as broadly as possible. The office also directly administers programs with universitywide constituencies, such as the state and city government internship programs and the University Year for Action program.

Thus far, the focus of the office has been on working with colleges and departments, through the new Council on Experiential Education, to encourage them to build experiential education into the curriculum. At the same time, interdisciplinary subcommittees are also at work devising ways in which the off-campus placement can be utilized to encourage department cooperation (for example, a subcouncil for cultural patterns consists of representatives from anthropology, English folklore, geography, sociology, and history).

Efforts have also gone into cataloguing all the university field experience programs and all the university courses being used to grant credit for field work. Research has been conducted on income taxes, workman's compensation, and minimum wage requirements.

The Office for Experiential Education exists in an environment which is generally tolerant if not wholly enthusiastic about its mission. There remains a considerable degree of academic conventionalism, a fear of eroding standards, an anxiety about the theft of credit as though it were gold being burgled out of some academic Fort Knox. The words of the poet who penned "The Deserted Campus" represent this point of view eloquently:

CREDIT, thou elder brother e'en to grade,
Thou hadst a being ere degrees were made,
When to have ta'en a course meant mastering
A discipline–not doing one's own thing!
To what base uses has thy name been lent,
Thou tarnish'd token of accomplishment!
For credit they cross seas, pay gladly double

To learn what they could here with half the trouble.
For credit they watch plays, or hammer nails,
Or get a clap, or hunt for Holy Grails;
They'll lobby Congress, or their boots they'll muddy,
If certifi'd as independent study,
And though we fume, we pedagogues abet it;
Ingenious are the ways of earning credit:
They ski in Zermatt and they scour the pampas,
They'll do most anything but stay on campus.*

Major Projects. Two current efforts may provide a better test of the office's ability to function. One of these is to steer course credit for experiential learning (up to thirty hours) through each academic department and the faculty senate. Thus far, twenty-four departments have endorsed the concept of the course (presented through a "model" course proposal and argumentation). The adoption of this course by appropriate departments, and later the appointment of specific instructors for the course, will be a first tangible demonstration of success. The new course also carries with it the necessity of a written contract; thus experiential education has developed this tool and is working with students and faculty in its use.

Secondly, a major information center is being established for students who want field placement, modeled somewhat on the C/AHED (See-Ahead) Center at Michigan State University. The information center is seen as the only feasible way of dealing with hundreds of student inquiries without spending massive amounts of staff time in personal counseling.

Student Role. Yet the major objective, perhaps equally as important as faculty support, is that of creating within the student body both the interest in exploring off-campus opportunities and the willingness to aggressively develop off-campus experiences for themselves. As one means of achieving this, learning opportunities in Kentucky are being gathered together into something like a Whole Earth Catalogue. Hopefully, by attractively packaging this catalogue, and including written encouragement for students to experiment, we will at least start students on the path toward working independently.

This last point deserves digression and elaboration. It is be-

*Ira Gorshan, "The Deserted Campus," *Chronicle of Higher Education*, April 1, 1974.

coming fairly obvious that the students we deal with have not been encouraged to take charge of and actively pursue their own educations; they do not ask why they are here, what their learning goals are, or how they can best achieve their goals. In other words they have been schooled to be told what and how they are to learn. Experiential education, which depends on student independence and initiative, cannot thrive in this environment. Consequently, not only must we create an environment where students will think "off campus," but we need to cooperate with others on the campus who are attempting to revitalize undergraduate education and encourage more creative student attitudes toward the educational process.

Experiential Education in Liberal Arts. A corollary need, in our opinion, is to integrate experiential education into the general education program of the university. The professional schools, and in turn careerism, continue to be the mainstays of field experience. It is our opinion that it will be in the liberal arts fields that experiential learning can have its most significant impact. For it is here that the university continues to play its distinct role, not only as the keeper of the society's culture, but also as the place for helping develop men and women who can cope with society's complex ethical and cultural problems and who can lead personally satisfying and socially constructive lives as citizens in a participatory democracy. So we have considered that by combining liberal arts values with field placements, a new breath of life might be blown into an old academic objective. If learning by doing is a concept valid for engineers, why is it not appropriate for all decision-making citizens? If understanding the internal workings of organizations like government is a desirable object for all educated persons, as well as political scientists, why not use the experiential technique to convey the message of the humanities?

Cost/Benefit Analysis. Another need, which will be more obvious to administrators at higher levels than ourselves, is to cost our efforts to determine whether our efforts are worth the price. The Office for Experiential Education at the University of Kentucky obviously will not become institutionalized until its costs are known and are felt to be reasonable and affordable in view of the benefits derived. How these benefits can be measured is a question yet to be answered to everyone's satisfaction.

The creation of the Office for Experiential Education at UK does not mean that "experiential education" has been institutionalized at the university; it says only that an institution has been created with the goal of institutionalizing the concept. Only the first step has been taken; the most important goals lie ahead. Until the university, with full awareness and agreement, finally understands what it has done by creating this office and understands the implications of experiential learning as they relate to goals long held to be important in higher education, experiential education will not be institutionalized.

Robert F. Sexton is the executive director of the Office for Experiential Education at the University of Kentucky. He was the Director of Intern Programs for Kentucky, a founder and chairman of the board of directors of the National Center for Public Service Internship Programs, and a member of the steering committee of the Society for Field Experience Education.
John B. Stephenson is dean of undergraduate studies and associate professor of sociology at the University of Kentucky. As dean, Stephenson has had an opportunity to apply abstract principles to the practice of change, in pursuit of such goals as the improvement of instruction and advising and the development of alternative teaching-learning models.

The overall concerns of program design are dealt with, including funding, academic credit, and program administration.

program design

frank d. van aalst

There are four main thrusts within Field Experience Education (FEE): off-campus research, career exploration, community service, and intercultural experience. These different objectives are not mutually exclusive; they can be combined in a variety of ways. Most FEE programs have a research element, and also recognize the educational value of experience. Different parties to the same program may have different goals. The student may be motivated to test a career, while the community agency values the service contribution and the faculty supervisor waits to see the final research paper. Even though these need not be contradictory, it can be confusing and potentially harmful to a program if the different parties are not clearly aware of differences in expectations. The strongest program is probably one in which a particular emphasis is clearly articulated but others are recognized as valid secondary objectives. It is also possible to design an umbrella structure under which diversity is defined and encouraged.

Of the four emphases, two, community service and intercultural experience, have developed significantly during the past decade. Facilitated by the Southern Regional Education Board (SREB), the service-learning concept has found expression in numerous places in the South. The National Center for Public Service Internships, the Center for Washington Learning Opportunities, and an increasing number of state and city government internship programs are all engaged in the development of service-learning. Many ACTION projects are now being integrated with university FEE programs. In recent years community service programs have been fastest growing, and most of what follows in this paper is primarily applicable to this type.

Intercultural experience is the focus of required off-campus components at Justin Morrill (Michigan State) and Merrill College (Santa Cruz). In both of these, preparation and follow-up seminars are basic elements. Johnston College (Redlands) and New College Oakland (Michigan) have similar emphases. Established international study programs now tend to emphasize the experiential component as integral rather than peripheral.

There are many diversified programs deliberately established, or umbrella offices to coordinate a variety of existing but unrelated programs. Colleges with a FEE requirement, like Goddard and Beloit, usually permit a wide range of choice in project types as does St. Mary's College of Maryland. Some larger institutions have developed central coordinative offices which have built up some momentum of their own such as the Off Campus Term Program at the University of South Florida. UCLA and the University of Kentucky are developing overall FEE plans. On many large campuses various departments have their separate off-campus programs. The most diversified of all FEE organizations is the North Carolina Internship Office which coordinates, facilitates, and develops a wide variety of programs at colleges and universities throughout the state.

All involve at least three parties: the student, a faculty and/or administrative supervisor, and a receiving organization (community or field) supervisor. The successful program requires a dynamic interchange among all the participants. When the initiative has come from above (the governor's office or the state legislature or the college president's office), there is an immediate advantage in avoiding bureaucratic obstacles but a disadvantage if responsibility for implementation is not clearly assigned.

The North Carolina Internship Office includes student initiative-building as a main goal. A number of other programs, like those at New College Hofstra and Merrill College (Santa Cruz), put a heavy initial burden on the student to petition a committee with a clear proposal for his self-designed project. An element of this is a good component for any program.

academic credit

The major policy issue affecting FEE is whether it deserves academic credit in a liberal arts context. Professional and technical education both have their internships, apprenticeships, and practica. The burgeoning community colleges provide career training for the paraprofessionals. The liberal arts institutions do provide career training for the academic profession but many students are in that increasingly restless group who feel that they are obliged to mark time before going on to something worthwhile, whether it be graduate school or the job market.

FEE advocates have used a variety of themes. The field is real life where the student is confronted with the demands of an adult world. Experience is the best teacher and raises different types of questions, which affect the student as a person rather than just an intellect. This result has as much educational value as what normally goes on in the classroom, if not more. FEE tackles the problem of lifelong learning styles by combining work and formal learning in a single setting. In contrast to the normal notion that work is in the community and learning on campus, FEE requires an academic paper based on what is learned on a job and is of value to the employer. In this is the potential for integrating two basic human activities that have been unfortunately and unnaturally separated.

The value of the whole comes in the student's reflection on what is happening and his formulation of what he is learning in a manner which can be communicated to others. To facilitate this whole learning process the student ideally keeps a journal, writes a major paper, and writes an evaluation. Each of these represents an essential step in a holistic learning process that can become a lifelong style. The journal is a record of what happens to me, and how I am growing. The paper is some academic project presented in a form acceptable to both the professional and academic world. In a formal evaluation the student joins with his supervisors in discussing his own and the others' roles. For this total program, academic credit can be defended.

Regular jobs do not offer the opportunity for this kind of learning experience. FEE is as much a challenge to the receiving organization as to the academic institution. For the experience to be relevant to the student's academic program, and a satisfactory career exploration, the student should be able to learn some specific skills, be shown the overall operation, observe the decision-making process, participate at least at a paraprofessional level, and complete a special project. This is no easy task to accomplish in a semester! It requires an experienced professional willing and able to be a teacher giving the student a more responsible role each week. A clue to success is finding a qualified individual in a responsible position to be community supervisor. Serious consideration must be given to how best to recognize and reward the qualified supervisor by giving him/her some kind of faculty status.*

Such reasons are used to justify the granting of full academic credit for full-time off-campus learning. A few institutions grant this credit in a single block, others as pieces for different parts of the whole: for example, two for practicum; four for keeping a journal evaluating an experience; four for participating in a full evening seminar each week with other off-campus students; four for a research paper; two for writing a final evaluation. It is easier for a student to get partial credit in this arrangement should some aspect of the FEE go sour but it also weakens its integrative nature. Another practice is a variable credit policy, whereby an approving committee assesses the credit value of each specific student proposal. This evaluation can be done prior to the experience or after the fact. There is the possibility of beginning with the assumption that the FEE is only worth about half-time credit as has been traditionally true of laboratory sessions. In each case the student's fees will be determined by the amount of credit agreed upon.

Should the credit be applicable to major requirements? What is the total amount of FEE credit applicable toward a degree? Can a student do two years of public service internships and fulfill all his upper-division requirements for a B.A. in political science? Most programs are focused on juniors, who have more maturity but can still come back to enrich the classroom. Receivers prefer the student close to graduation to increase the possibility of recruiting the good intern for a regular job. The intern often likes it this way also. Placing freshmen and sophomores runs the risk of fostering a restlessness that makes it very difficult for them to stick out the time required to get the degree. There is considerable diversity in practice.

It is difficult to give full credit if there is not some formal, traditional product (an academic paper). It is equally true that it is perhaps impossible to supervise a FEE program that is not full time and granted full credit. Credit hours produce Full-Time Equivalencies, the currency of higher education. Anything less than full credit simply cannot buy the amount of supervisory time required.

*Such a learning process tackles the question of relationship between the liberal arts and career preparation head on. This area is wide open for experimentation and analysis.

funding

The funding picture remains chaotic. Off-campus programs are wide open to abuse. The agency can get cheap labor, the student can get double remuneration, and the college can collect tuition without providing instructional services.

ITEM: The student pays a tuition fee; for that he deserves full instructional service. So for every seventeen (or whatever the student-faculty ratio happens to be) students off campus there is the equivalent of one full-time faculty person available for academic supervision of the FEE program.

ITEM: The agency gets a full-time employee. But if he is given access to an overview of the agency's operations, is free to ask questions, is given help in the collection of materials for a research paper, and is given regular supervision by the agency, then the agency is providing an instructional service as well. The FEE student makes certain demands on the agency; he reimburses the agency by providing his services. Hopefully, he will give a bit more than he receives.

The Massachusetts Internship Office made it clear: you work for credit or money, not both. The SREB programs have recognized that a full salary puts the student in an employee relationship with the agency and have suggested amounts in the neighborhood of $75.00 per week, with the clear understanding with the agency that the student is to be more than an employee. In cooperative education programs, where the student is regularly employed and salaried, only token academic credit is given if at all.

While it may not be good policy to make FEE financially rewarding, it also should not create additional financial burdens for the average student. A good goal is to make it no more expensive than if the student were taking regular courses on campus. Here are some relevant observations:

1. By remaining enrolled in college as a full-time student, most scholarships (such as senatorial and VA benefits) can still be received.
2. Work-study money can be used in service-learning programs so the qualifying student need not lose that resource.
3. There are still some Office of Education Institute of International Studies Group Program funds, and other HEW funds potentially available for special projects.
4. Some federal funds are available for training of professionals and subprofessionals in public administration.

5. The Student Intern Project of the Southern Regional Education Board has been supported by a grant from the Office of Economic Research, Economic Development Administration, U.S. Department of Commerce.
6. If the student lives away from campus, the business office may be persuaded to waive extra fees (such as student activities).
7. Most agencies will be able to provide mileage for use of a car on the job.
8. Some students may live at home if their internship is nearby.
9. Some agencies may have resources to pay the student an amount to defray extra expenses. If FEE were made a state policy, all state agencies could have interns included in their budgets.
10. Special scholarships can be solicited from interested community persons.
11. As community groups recognize the value of interns they can include intern stipends in their budget projections.
12. Private enterprise may want an intern and be willing to pay the equivalent of a full salary to the program which could then be distributed to interns according to need.

In the present economic climate it is probably wise to design programs that will not require special program funding for implementation. At the same time any academic institution must be willing to invest at least as much per student in FEE as it does in the other institutional programs.

administration

The administration question is related to finance. There is a temptation for the program designers to leave the details up to the persons directly involved: the student and his two supervisors. But the experience is an unusual one for all of them, and unless someone has an overview there is little chance for success. In the same fashion that a college determines administrative overhead per student credit hour, at least that amount of administrative service should be available for the FEE program, and in its developmental stage, a bit more.

When FEE is a stated objective of the institution, whether required or available to all who choose, the task of the responsible officer is much easier than when FEE is peripheral to the main purpose of the institution or is supported by a single department as a special project. But even a lavishly funded, diversified program is weakened if it is alien to the curriculum. In other words, there must be both administrative and faculty support for a successful program. It is recommended that FEE be integral to the curricular design, not a special interest program with a special staff. The faculty supervision ideally comes from regular faculty, with assignments made in the same way as are other teaching assignments.

Most FEE programs are designed as supportive to established majors, and some require that the off-campus experience be related to the student major. But those stressing intercultural experiences are frequently seen by students as providing a liberating experience not available in their restrictive major programs. It is immediately apparent that full-time off-campus programs are possible only when there is at least a minimal flexibility in curriculum design. A student must be able to take all the required courses for a major in seven semesters. Such variables are the institutional realities into which the program must fit. Similar issues are evident in receiving organizations.

A coordinator-interpreter must get the parties together and keep them together. Finally, he has to bring together the pieces of evaluation. It is possible for a receiving agency to provide this service and justify cost in terms of student services rendered in a service type program. It is also possible for a broker to perform this function, to be paid by any one of the other parties. This payment should be made by the college or university which has accepted the student's tuition fee and has agreed to grant credit.

If no credit is granted, we are dealing with volunteer service or straight employment or foreign travel, not FEE. It thus seems difficult to design an adequate FEE program without the educational institution's providing administrative services. These may be on a consortium basis, as the Great Lakes College Association International Studies programs, or a state college system, but they must exist somewhere. The requirements for creating and maintaining a program are numerous.

1. Clarification of the educational goal(s) of the program, including its relationship with the curriculum.
2. Formulation of policy on academic credit and acceptance by appropriate bodies.
3. Allocation of administrative and instructional resources at least equivalent to the cost per credit hour of regular curricular programs.
4. Job descriptions from receiving agencies.
5. Definition of roles of both college and community supervisors.

6. Articulation of educational expectations by students.
7. Interview between receiving agency and student.
8. Clarification of student's academic responsibilities.
9. A written agreement (learning contract) signed by all major parties, focusing on the educational goals and means of achievement in terms of the responsibilities of each party to the agreement. It seems preferable to incorporate all in a single document even though it is possible to have the student sign separate agreements with his/her college and community supervisors. Hours of work, holidays, and all financial agreements should be included.
10. Explicit means of evaluation.
11. Provision for observation by administration and settling of misunderstandings in emergency situations.

In virtually all of the above matters, the need for administrative resources is obvious. FEE is a serious educational development with as yet unrealized potential for improvement in higher education. There is now enough groundwork laid to be able to draw up the design for a sound program. There are no shortcuts. Clear commitment of all institutions involved is essential. And on the college/university side there is no escape from the commitment of both instructional and administrative time.

FEE and innovation

FEE is one product of the innovative movement in higher education in the 1960s. The pioneer programs were in experimental institutions like New College Sarasota, or in experimental units of large universities, such as Justin Morrill at Michigan State, New College at Oakland or at Hofstra, Merrill College at Santa Cruz or Livingston College at Rutgers. That their survival rate has been good is due to a number of factors.

First, FEE incorporates in sharply focused programs a wide variety of innovative educational ideas and concerns. It stresses affective development, it recognizes the educational value of experience, it provides relevant and practical education, it prepares for new vocations, it employs contract learning, and it has many of the characteristics of a university without walls.

At the same time FEE has been seen as constructive by state legislators, because it places students in established, real life, adult situations. To concerned students and parents it is seen as a serious grappling with the relation between liberal arts and careers.

Probably the main clue to its success is the simple fact that it does not threaten the whole institution. It can provide a place for innovation in the midst of a relatively traditional curriculum. It may be accurate to say that FEE is the main focal point of the lasting results of the innovative sixties. It may also be a continuing means to change the whole structure of higher liberal arts education.

Frank D. van Aalst is professor of history and director of Off Campus Learning at St. Mary's College of Maryland. He was formerly chairman of the social science division. Prior to that he taught for five years at the University of Rajasthan in Jaipur, India.

The evolutionary and nontraditional format of experiential education has resulted in a variety of techniques for assessing the learning of individual students.

evaluating experiential education

edward l. angus

If one asked the question, What does one want to learn, the next question would be how best to learn it. Four modes of learning come readily to mind: the traditional classroom/teacher; meditation; observation; and experience. Each may be appropriate for the learning task and the individual involved at a particular time. Also although the current organization of public education seems to ignore the fact, all people do not learn in the same way, nor do they consider what is offered to be learned as consistently appropriate with their individual needs. In contrast to classroom education, experientially based education generally demands that the learner establish his own learning agenda, where and how he will learn. That fact may be one of the significant factors involved in recent increased interest in experiential learning. It is also at the core of the innovative movement in education today, and a source of difficulty in evaluating field experience education.

This paper addresses the particular problem of how to evaluate experientially based learning, focusing on individual field learning experiences. I am not here concerned with evaluation for purposes of awarding academic credit for prior experiences. The context of this discussion is the service-learning model of field-based learning. In this situation the project or task on which the intern is working is meeting some public need. The student is receiving academic credit and probably some financial remuneration. Ideally, the intern is devoting full-time (forty hours a week for ten to fifteen weeks) to the internship, although other time arrangements might easily fall within this paper's scope.

Purpose. Evaluation generally has two objectives: to evaluate the student's performance as to skill development, knowledge and experience acquisition and work accomplished and to evaluate the effectiveness of the various elements of the total program in accomplishing its goals.

valuable program components assuring effective evaluation

Clearly Defined Objectives. As with all education, clearly defined objectives are a necessity if any effective evaluation is to be accomplished. The participants in a particular experiential education project must agree to a set of specific learning objectives before the project begins. Without such goals, it is virtually impossible to evaluate the experience objectively. Ideally, these learning objectives should be generated by the student in collaboration with the appropriate faculty and agency personnel. The faculty member should see that the learning objectives are pedagogically sound and the agency's role is to ensure that the task element of the experience meets a public need.

Research by Kiel (1972) has substantiated that the clearer the learning objectives the greater the likelihood of a personally and intellectually fulfilling experience for the student. And if the task is meaningful to the student, his motivation is enhanced. Only the individual can learn; others may facilitate that learning but the desire to know originates within each person. Objectives serve to clarify the learning process. Needless to say, unanticipated events or consequences may occur during the field placement that alter the original objectives and such should not be overlooked in the evaluative process. Indeed, experiential education provides many more opportunities for accidental and incidental learning than do other modes, and this is seen as one of the strengths of that mode in moving students from being dependent to becoming independent learners.

Prefield Orientation. In order that students will know what is expected of them, what will be evaluated and how, and will be helped to maximize the learning potential available through the field experience a prefield orientation is valuable. One means is a workshop that stresses such themes as problem-solving techniques, failure expectation level, or decision-making skills. Another way is to assemble written, audio, and video materials in a learning resources center on subjects such as those just mentioned. A third approach is curricular. A course or parts of several courses that lead up to a field experience will serve to maximize its impact; for example, courses or modules might deal with research methods, interviewing techniques, operation of sophisticated audio or video equipment, organizational theory, a course in state and local government, folklore, or minority studies. The prefield orientation is held as soon as students can be brought together after their assignment. Length of the preparation depends on need. In my view, if a school or department is seriously committed to exposing a significant number of students to experiential education, part of the commitment ought to include mechanisms for prefield orientation. Evidence of the utility of such sessions may be found in specific professional programs, such as social work and teacher preparation, that include orientation and field experiences as part of the degree program.

The importance of prefield preparation to the evaluative process is that students can be expected to derive certain skills and knowledge as well as realistic expectations of the field experience. Final evaluations concerning field performance can then be made in light of the prefield training.

Individualized Learning Contract and Reading List. In the service-learning model of field experience education, as in others, the individualized learning contract is widely used. This permits and assures that the learning opportunities provided by a particular placement are identified and the learning objectives clearly specified. This clear specification of objectives makes evaluation possible and provides a means by which the relationship between theory and practice can be explored more fully. Such a contract is best developed by the student and his faculty advisor in consultation with the agency supervisor. Often included in the learning contract will be a reading list and some reporting mechanism for evaluation purposes. The importance and usefulness of readings lie in raising questions in the student rather than simply increasing general knowledge of some subject matter.

Evaluation of Student Performance. What follows is a report on some of the best practices I know about in evaluating student performance in field experience education. Used alone, no technique would provide sufficient evaluative information. These relevant methods are mostly nontraditional in the sense of the prevailing model of education.

1. *Intermediate feedback.* Periodic on-site visitations by the faculty advisor or field project director can serve as ongoing evaluation, provide corrective and/or motivational feedback, and assess some aspects of intellectual growth. Site visits can also provide information on the supervisor's attitudes and the student's relationships with other employees, as well as a check on adherence to the initial goals. If the learning objectives appear altered, corrective measures can be taken or revised objectives negotiated. Such adjustments are essential so that the final evaluation is related to the actual field experience. Periodic meetings, perhaps back on campus if convenient, between the student and the faculty advisor can also serve many of the same purposes as well as other more academic ones. For example, discussions of reading materials or literature that relate to the experience as well as frank assessments by the student may be the format of such meetings. These meetings should not replace on-site visits, however, for in addition to the value of seeing the situation for oneself, such visits by a faculty person reaffirm the educational worth of the field experience to both the student and the agency personnel. "He cared enough to come and see me." If visits are simply impossible, periodic written reports or even telephone conversations with the student and agency supervisor may accomplish similar results.

2. *Seminars or workshops during the field experience.* "In-service" workshops involving groups of interns are prevalent. While a variety of formats for such sessions are used, general components would include the following. One or more faculty members, students, or possibly agency personnel would have responsibility for the meetings. Reading lists, duplicated materials, lectures, and discussions that relate to the field placement or to a body of knowledge relevant to the experiences are used. For example, one of the largest political internship programs, that of the CUNY system, includes seminars with readings and discussions focused on specific problems or ideas, such as executive decision making, strategies for change, or the theory and practice of community power. The group meets for several hours one or more times during the period of the field experience. This technique stresses relating a body of knowledge to the experience (emphasizing the experiential learning dimension) and encourages participants to reflect on and contrast their personal (concrete) experiences with the more conceptually abstract literature. A variant would be to use these sessions for skill development in areas of felt need.

3. *Critical incident writing.* This technique, described earlier in this issue by Duley, is not widely utilized but I find it impressive. The Justin Morrill program provides an excellent description of this evaluative device. Students are required to submit (in writing) to the program director nine critical incident reports at the conclusion of their field study. These describe specific situations and actions taken that demonstrate the utilization of what are termed cross-cultural skills. According to Morrill field study materials: "Since the critical incidents are descriptions of individual students' behavior they can also provide the students opportunities to examine their own values (by values here is meant virtues, principles, beliefs, convictions, comforts, material possessions, and desires [desires for money, power, position, influence, status, education and the respect of others] which are so important to the student that they strongly influence or determine his decisions and behavior) and how these affect their behavior. These reflections then become occasions for gaining self-knowledge."

4. *Maintaining a diary or journal.* The keeping of a daily journal or diary is a technique with both educational and evaluative worth. I have found that most students need fairly strong urging to keep up their journals and not be discouraged because their initial entries are not "pearls of wisdom" or brilliant insights into theretofore unsolved problems. However, a well-kept journal, periodically reviewed and discussed by the intern and faculty counselor, can add significantly to the learning process. Like critical incident writing, reflections recorded in a journal also generate knowledge of self.

5. *Exit interview or final written evaluation.* The use of exit interviews or written evaluations by both the agency supervisor and the faculty counselor furnish useful immediate feedback for the student. A final interview can provide immediate rewards for the student and serve as a legitimation of a task accomplished. Discussions of the experience and constructive criticism by and of each of the three parties involved can stimulate the learning process while the experience is still fresh in all their minds. If a formal written evaluation is made of the student by either the supervisor or the faculty member, a discussion of that evaluation with the student may accomplish similar goals.

6. *Was the job well done?* This is a less formal procedure than the one indicated above but nonetheless a useful one. It is to ask the simple question, "Was the job well done?" Asked of the student, the faculty advisor, and the agency supervisor, along with why or why not, it will generate considerable evidence.

7. *Written or final reports.* Several types of final reports are

in use. One is a written report in a form useful to the agency in which the student served. Such a report can serve as the focus of the student's work task. A second type is a final self-analysis (either written or oral) of the student's behavior and learning during and as a result of the field experience. Periodic or progress reports are also common. They stimulate the intern to reflect periodically on progress toward stated goals. A fourth type of assessment is a group evaluation by peers of a student's report on the field experience.

8. *Examinations.* If cognitive mastery of an area is a principal concern and can be clearly identified as a result of the field experience, as examination or a series of tests is used to determine the student's competency.

9. *Return or post-field experience seminars.* Depending upon academic credit and course structures, post-field seminars may be a day or two of sessions at the conclusion of the field experience in which students reflect and report on their personal experiences or they may extend for a more lengthy period. Justin Morrill College, for example, uses the latter and their return seminar, the third of a three-semester sequence, focuses on values clarification. Merrill College (U.C., Santa Cruz) provides a variety of post-field options, including opportunities to speak to classes, work with students in pre-field orientations, or take specific courses relating closely to the field experience. Colleges using a post-field seminar clearly think that the learning dimensions of the field experience are maximized in this setting. There is little doubt that when a group of students who have had very diverse field experiences get together, there is vast potential for exploring various relationships, values clarification, and integrating the field experience with other courses, experiences, or bodies of knowledge.

10. *Self-evaluation.* Having the student do some serious reflection—what occurred, if and how values conflicts arose and were resolved, what was learned and how that related to other learning situations—can help him place the field experience in perspective. Discussions of such an evaluation between the faculty advisor and student can serve to further highlight the learning that resulted.

Program Evaluation. The performance of students is not the only thing being evaluated in field experience education. Programs are being evaluated also. A number of survey instruments are in use to assess the learning opportunities provided and the consequences of the programs for students. A rather generalized form, developed by David Kiel for the North Carolina Internship Office, evaluates learning opportunities provided by a service-learning internship.

Other types of questionnaires are being developed to provide more specific data in such areas of concern as cost per credit hour, appropriate faculty load, contribution of the field placement to the total educational experience of the student, the impact of the program on the student's career or professional goal clarification. Instruments are also being developed to ascertain the extent of value clarification and cultural understanding which occurred as a result of the program. Longitudinal studies are being used to assess the long range impact of field experience education by following up students four to five years after graduation.

The student is not the only learner; supervisors and faculty also participate in the learning experience. If nothing is happening in the advisor's and the supervisor's head and heart, the learning situation is probably inadequate. How to determine this may be difficult, but a few questions asked of students, faculty, and agency supervisors about programs are: Did the supervisor and advisor raise "hard" questions for the intern; were they receptive to new ideas or ways of doing things; did they provide a workable task and a supportive environment for its accomplishment; and did they engage the student in searches for alternative paths to problem solving? Like students, not all supervisors or faculty advisors are natural inquirers and some, if not most, will need assistance in further developing those skills. Workshops or other sessions can be a definite asset in this area. (The North Carolina Internship Office "Internship Style Description Form" has been found to be helpful in such workshops, particularly for goals clarification. Also, their publication "Skills for Effective Supervision of Interns" and "Skills for Effective Faculty Counseling of Service-Learning Interns" are useful tools.)

conclusion

As stated earlier, few if any of the above techniques by themselves will provide an adequate evaluation of field experience, and each program director or faculty member involved in evaluating and credentialing experiential education has certain local criteria to satisfy. Much remains to be accomplished in providing sufficient empirically based evidence for any single technique. It is my experience that the evolving nature of experiential education on many college campuses has caused continual shifts in emphasis. Because experiential education is nontraditional, innovative assessment techniques might serve best. At the same time, as Hedlund (1973, p. 8) has pointed out so succinctly, "greater effort must be made to communicate the findings and the results of theory-testing–theory building." For that to occur, more careful attention must be given to documenting the evaluative techniques employed. Although their concern is not unique in education today, those involved in field experience education are anxious to test and develop a theoretical base for experiential learning.

references

Hedlund, R. D. "Internship Evaluation: A Review and Proposal." *Public Service Internship News,* May-June, 1973, 5-8.

Kiel, D. H. *Student Learning Through Community Involvement.* Atlanta: Southern Regional Education Board, 1972.

Edward L. Angus is associate professor of social and behavioral sciences and director of institutional research at Mars Hill College, Mars Hill, North Carolina. As a participant in experiential education, he was an administrative intern in the office of Tennessee Governor Frank Clement, spent two summers as a staff member of the Resource Development Internship Project at the Southern Regional Education Board, and directed the Community Development Institute and the Academic Internship Program at Mars Hill.

To establish successful ongoing experiential learning programs one must Instigate, Introduce, Interpret, Implement, and continuously Inspect the undertaking.

organizing innovation: five stages

william r. o'connell, jr.
w. edmund moomaw

> At the summit true politics and strategy are one. The manoeuvre which brings an ally into the field is as serviceable as that which wins a great battle.
>
> Winston Churchill
> *The World Crisis*

Three concerns arise in the process of successfully initiating and running a self-sustaining, off-campus experiential educational program: gaining approval or acceptance for the establishment and continuance of such a program; organizing the program; and creating relationships among various people and programs within a particular geographical area or across the nation.

Organizing a campus innovation such as off-campus learning seems to incorporate a unique set of elements. For this presentation we have developed what we call "the five I's of innovation organization." To establish successful on-going experiential learning one must Instigate, Introduce, Interpret, Implement, and continuously Inspect the undertaking.

instigation

To develop a new program, the idea may be proposed by someone off the campus or through several techniques within the institution. Many years of experience of the Southern Regional Education Board (SREB) and similar agencies has demonstrated that the role of the "outside agent" is extremely important in instigating and developing organizational structures for off-campus experiential education. We believe this technique is effective, speedy, and most useful in establishing self-sustaining independent programs. Since the very nature of "off-campus learning" involves persons both inside and outside the institution, some agent or organization capable of bringing these two environments together is critical because there usually is no previous basis for a working relationship. The recent expansion of service-learning opportunities in the South attests to the importance of this concept.

The outside agent stimulus can occur at various levels. An agency such as SREB working in conjunction with a foundation or federal program or agency can accomplish objectives in a broad geographical area—in this case a fourteen-state region. SREB can then serve as the outsider to stimulate program development within a state or at a substate or multiinstitutional level.

As the outside agent providing the impetus for service-learning programs in the South, SREB made a variety of approaches to regents, administrators, professors, and government leaders. In West Virginia, program planning and initiation are taking place at the level of the chancellor of the board of regents; in Tennessee the beginning stages are in the governor's office; in Alabama one institution is laying the groundwork, and in Florida the process involved a combination of participants, with faculty and administrators from several institutions, representatives from the board of regents, the legislature, and the governor's office all joining together to plan a statewide program.

A major influence wielded by the outside agent is money. We cannot minimize the concerns about funding expressed by academic administrators, agency heads, and government officials. In many cases a lack, or perceived lack, of funds is the automatic reason, excuse, or justification for not considering a new idea or a change in the usual way of doing things. Even a few dollars which can serve as tangible evidence that a suggested idea is "worth something" will stimulate movement far faster than many hours of persuasion about the inherent values of the idea proposed. However, the amount of money is not the most important factor we have seen in the South, and few dollars have stimulated great expansion of off-campus learning opportunities far beyond that developed earlier with many thousands of dollars more.

At another level there is stimulation for program development in the institution itself. Programs can get started in various ways, but in every case an individual or group must serve as a focal point on the campus. One of several approaches might be used.

The instigation might come from an *internal independent innovator,* an individual or a team which takes the lead in developing or proposing a new program. This person or group usually has enough independence, individual influence, or control over a small area to undertake and put a program into operation.

Another approach might be through an *appointed institutional leader.* In this instance the person or team providing the leadership or focus for development might be acting for the institution. They may have received a commission or at least approval from an appropriate internal power figure to begin this effort. For example, the administration may have decided that the internship concept is a good one and wants an influential person to demonstrate it for the rest of the institution.

The external influence-support approach is yet another way to instigate the idea. The institutional person or team may have been stimulated to try out the idea by someone or some agency off-campus. This agent may have convinced the person or team of a good idea, the agent may have political or public influence, or the agent may offer financial support or reward for the individuals or team or for the institutional program. Under these circumstances the program may be encouraged or at least tolerated or allowed on the campus because of the outside relationship, especially in the beginning phase.

The various forms of instigation we have discussed are not mutually exclusive. More than one might be used, several might exert influences simultaneously, and any one might influence either or all of the others. This is, in fact, the most exciting aspect of such efforts—the continuing, dynamic development at all levels as a result of the cyclic, revolving, continuous interaction of the various components.

introduction

Once the idea has been "planted" and the contacts established to carry forward the development, the program can be introduced by a demonstration or pilot effort. The demonstration of the idea can be quite small, taking place in only one department of one college, or it can be quite large, perhaps operating at the state level through a governor's office, depending on the ultimate operating unit envisioned.

Of the several programs now operating statewide in the South, a variety of introductory approaches and techniques were used. In Virginia the pilot program was operated by the higher education coordinating agency; in South Carolina, Georgia, and Texas the programs were started through the governors' offices. In North Carolina, the office was set up jointly by the State Office of Administration and the higher education system. North Carolina, Georgia, and South Carolina began with a large number of students in the introductory program while Texas had only twelve interns the first year.

In states where institutions have been encouraged to join the service-learning efforts, various institutional approaches also have been used. At the University of North Carolina-Charlotte the program began under the auspices of the Urban Institute and received endorsement and support from the top administrative level. In each of several Texas institutions the service-learning program was introduced through a single faculty member identified and hired by the state program because he or she had a reputation for being interested in this approach to learning.

interpretation

Interpretation of the pilot or demonstration is crucial to generate enthusiastic support from persons both on and off campus who will influence further direction, adoption, and support. The effort must be highly publicized around those who need to be involved. The interpretation must include clear-cut information about the value of the undertaking, what it set out to do, how it was accomplished, and the means of moving from the pilot to the full operational state. In addition, role determinations and a network of working relationships among persons on and off campus must be established where close cooperative working relationships rarely have existed before.

Approval must be gained from the faculty and administrative officials but there is a major need to foster a spirit of experimentation and innovation within the institution. A matter of great concern to faculty is academic validity. Most educators accept as valid individual learning experiences off-campus which can be evaluated by traditional methods such as tests or term papers. Problems arise, however, when educators are asked to consider credit for field work which is not susceptible to being measured in the usual manner. For example, the learning benefits derived from a community-based experience with a strong service-learning emphasis are elusive for many educators. In the traditional institution, the need is to move beyond the conceptualization which accepts only an off-campus "laboratory-type" experience in which the student is merely field-testing the concepts and theories learned in the classroom. Internships and field activities for students in political science, sociology, anthropology, and psychology generally are being recognized as academically valid because the experience is provided to amplify the classroom. But in using the term "off-campus experiential education," we refer to learning in addition to and complementary to the classroom, rather than merely an amplification of it, although certainly not a total replacement for classroom work. Educators must be asked to think of experiential learning in the framework of the total purposes of education as opposed to the narrower purposes of a specific course or a specific major. The goals achieved in the non-traditional off-campus experience point in the direction of developing the whole person—his own life style, his capacity for reflection, his knowledge of human concerns as well as his personal and academic skills.

Besides traditional faculty attitudes toward curriculum change, the matters of how much academic credit should be granted, what the faculty member's role is, how this role fits into the overall teaching load, and funding arrangements and techniques are complex issues that must be approached with an open and creative mind in each local setting.

Since the off-campus experiential program is a vital part of the student's educational development and part of his academic program, he should receive credit toward his degree objectives. Therefore, he requires and deserves the faculty attention and assistance he would normally receive. However, it is difficult for many educators to see what the professor's role might be vis à vis the student participating in that experience. When we speak of faculty assistance, we do not necessarily mean the traditional faculty member giving the traditional assistance. Perhaps the term "faculty" can be re-defined to mean "facilitator," or "partner in learning," and, if so, the problems of faculty definitions, faculty time, and faculty load can be dealt with in several other ways. The role of the faculty member is a vital one, however. The faculty advisor helps the student plan, perform, and reflect on his activities so that he achieves the greatest possible benefits. To encourage faculty to participate in these programs in a meaningful way, the traditional reward structure in academia may have to be revised. Most institutions have expected faculty to work with student intern experience in addition to their regular class loads and traditional responsibilities. The hours spent in the classroom can no longer be the sole basis for computing faculty loads. Advising, assisting, and evaluating students in non-classroom settings are becoming more significant aspects of the faculty member's job. Therefore, the basis for computing salaries should be revised to include these factors. Faculty loads also might be adjusted to allow time to prepare new learning experiences as well as to participate in them. A number of institutions now count new course preparation or the development of new ideas as equal to certain kinds of publications for promotion.

Administrators, legislators, and other educational leaders also need to reexamine current funding formulas and techniques so they can encourage rather than inhibit implementation of innovative programs and faculty participation. Funding formulas and financing procedures generally inhibit innovation because of the stress on traditional credit hours and "FTE's." New funding arrangements based on student outcomes rather than time may be the answer, but to date there is little experience with such procedures. In order to arrive at newer methods, arrangements should be made for programs to test outcome measures or some other financial base by providing special categories of funds for experimentation over a longer period of time. The strategy to be used here is to persuade the responsible people at all levels that the program is a valuable, vital part of the total institutional academic offering. The successful operation of the pilot or demonstration project will go a long way toward this end. Also, the involvement of an outside agent may be helpful at this point. The agent will be able to provide examples of successful programs elsewhere, including ways in which various hurdles have been overcome, and might also serve to bring together a number of persons who usually do not work together to solve such problems. One of the SREB efforts cited as most helpful in working with state programs is the ability of an influential outside agent to get program operations and institutional people together with policy makers at the system or state level. Another form of outside influence which can be used for persuasion is an existing network of off-campus experiential programs or advocates. The persons introducing the program can use such a network as evidence of the viability of the idea and its acceptability to similar institutions and people.

Off the campus, the program must be sanctioned by those who participate in providing the students' experiential situations. In the community-based experiential program, public agency and government officials and often community leaders must be involved and sometimes must provide financial support. These persons understand they are to participate in the student's academic program, but most must be convinced of the duality of the experience, since they usually only think of the service the student will perform.

In these instances two approaches are suggested. First, the agency or organization might be asked to look on their involvement as a contribution to the building of citizen awareness or to responsible citizen involvement in public affairs; as an opportunity to build desirable relationships among government personnel, young people, and educational institutions; and as a chance perhaps to recruit responsible young people into public service. A second approach is to emphasize that the student can provide a legitimate service to the agency as part of his educational experience. We have found in the South that the "project orientation," in which the student performs a specifically defined project for the public agency, is the most satisfactory arrangement for providing this service as part of the combined service-learning approach.

Once support or acceptance for the implementation of the program is achieved, the final obstacle is working out the relationships among all participants so that each will know what role he is to play. These relationships usually focus on the student as learner with the community-based person and the faculty advisor in supportive or guidance roles. But the total experience should be looked upon as a "partnership in learning," in which all parties participate in a cooperative relationship of mutual benefit to each person. From his own perspective, each participant defines specific tasks and immediate objectives, implements the project, provides feedback on progress, and develops additional learning opportunities. This kind of nontraditional program should not be hindered by traditional methods and role definitions. The issues must be approached with an open and creative mind to achieve the desired goals of off-campus learning.

implementation

After gaining the necessary approvals, the program can be implemented; that is, put into full operation as a part of the total institutional program. At this stage, the program will have been adopted formally by the college or university, roles will have been assigned, credit arrangements secured, financial arrangements settled, and the cycle of activity established. At the agency or governmental level all necessary legal or official arrangements will have been made.

During this implementation stage a network of relationships should be formally established with other fully operational programs, among a few institutions, statewide, regionally, or nationwide. Such networks might take various forms. Already existing consortia could develop cooperative experiential programs among their institutions as is now happening in Alabama; statewide college or university systems could operate joint experiential programs for their institution as is now proposed in West Virginia; a diverse category of institutions might join together to sponsor specialized or general experiential programs such as the Kentucky Administrative Internship Program and the Georgia Legislative Intern Program. Informal statewide alliances of institutions might be brought together under the sponsorship of a state government program, as in the Georgia and Texas internship programs, and institutions throughout a geographical region can and are forming informal alliances through internship programs sponsored by regional educational organizations. Finally, examples of possible beginning national networks including activities of the Society for Field Experience Education, the Center for Public Internship Programs, and the newly organized National Bicentennial Internship Program. Contact may have been made with such networks during the "Interpretation" stage to assist in overcoming obstacles to implementation, but once this stage has begun, formal relations should be initiated with existing networks, or new networks created. Such a cooperative organization is useful to:

–give a continuing and increasing legitimacy to each individual program through the joint relationship established;

–provide a continuing opportunity for the infusion and dissemination of new ideas and concepts into each individual program through the sharing of ideas and experiences by program directors and others;

–make available a more diverse selection of possible off-campus experiences for all students through the process of cross-placement among programs within the network;

–facilitate the growth and expansion of programs and the initiation of new programs by serving as one possible "outside agent" or "broker" available for instigation and consultation;

–help secure outside funding through information-sharing on funding sources and possible development of joint funding proposals.

A particularly important aspect of a network organization is that it can more readily sponsor new research into areas of experiential education than can an individual program. At present, for example, investigation is needed in the area of evaluation. Such research undertaken by a network organization would have more legitimacy and more likelihood of receiving the cooperative support and assistance necessary for a large undertaking. Moreover, the results would be more widely disseminated and more likely to receive wide acceptance than those produced by a single individual or program.

With "Implementation" the program should be considered fully institutionalized. It should then be allowed to run its cycle of activity long enough to determine its results. Judgments should not be made about its full operation until a sufficient number of experiences to have taken place.

inspection

The fifth and final phase of program development and operation is that of inspection, a continuous process of evaluation, questioning, and restructuring when necessary, to ensure the activity's permanence, its ability to meet or adapt to new conditions and circumstances, and its institutional acceptance. This stage begins a circular process in which new ideas and concepts lead to program readjustment or alteration, or even total program restructuring. Some or all the five stages of program development may need to be repeated. Being part of a network can assist in this stage through inter-program sharing, which provides a healthy atmosphere of evaluation and reevaluation. The "outside agent" also can be extremely helpful in reviewing and reporting on the program. Continuous inspection, within the program itself, by an outsider, or as part of a network of programs, will ensure each individual program's ability to adapt, to adjust, and to change with new conditions, or as new ideas and life styles require such change.

Off-campus experiential education has become a major and acceptable part of undergraduate education across the country. Stimulated partly by recommendations from national bodies such as the Carnegie Commission on Higher Education and the Newman Task Force, and given visibility by organizations such as SFEE, more and various types of institutions are adding activities outside the classroom and off the campus for many students. Growing acceptance on the part of educators, administrators, students, and government leaders has been stimulated by the increasing evidence of successful off-campus experiential programs which provide legitimate and significant learning experiences.

William R. O'Connell, Jr., is project director of the Undergraduate Education Reform Project of the Southern Regional Education Board. Previously, he was director of special programs of SREB. W. Edmund Moomaw is associate project director of the Undergraduate Education Reform Project of the Southern Regional Education Board. He was formerly director of the Student Intern Project of SREB.

Some answers to troubling questions:
Is it education? Can we pay for it?
How can we evaluate prior experience?

acceptability of field experience in traditional institutions

ernest a. lynton

The most crucial factor governing the degree of acceptability of field experience in traditional colleges and universities is the concept which the faculty members have individually about their own discipline and about their own scholarly work. The more they are oriented toward contemporary problems and issues of policy, the more readily will they recognize and indeed encourage the close relationship of practical experience to theoretical study.

sources of acceptance

A number of technical and professional fields have, of course, always included a period of clinical training as an integral part of their degree programs. Traditionally this field experience has come at the end of the course of study, reflecting a view of the curriculum as a series of sequential steps from science to application to clinical work. But in recent years there has been a growing recognition of the advantages of incorporating periods of practical involvement throughout the educational program as a way of bringing about optimal reinforcement between theory and application. (For a fuller discussion of this and related issues, see Schein, 1972, pp. 116-123.)

Such acceptance of the value of periods of field experience as a way to enhance a student's understanding of fundamental principles is fortunately not restricted to technical and professional fields. In one sense, it has of course always existed in the sciences, in which the laboratory has been an integral and essential part of both graduate and undergraduate curricula. Although in the vast majority of instances this laboratory work has been restricted to fragmented periods scattered throughout the more theoretical activities, the most prestigious institutions have always laid great stress on opportunities for periods of total research immersion, either on or off campus.

In recent years, there has been a growing recognition by faculty members in the social sciences and even in the humanities that their disciplines do not exist in a vacuum, and that practical experiences, properly structured and analyzed, can illuminate the methodology and principles of these fields. It would therefore seem to be an essential condition for the development of field experience on a significant scale, especially in a liberal arts institution, to have at least a few departments in which several faculty members relate their own scholarly and professional activities to practical applications. They would provide the nucleus of the group which would no longer ask whether field experience can have educational value, but would address itself to identifying the conditions under which this value is realized.

The first instinct of most such faculty members will be to follow—as in so many other ways—the example of their colleagues in the sciences, and to incorporate the equivalent of laboratory periods into the regular curriculum, interspersed with the regular courses and seminars. That approach has two advantages: it takes relatively little time away from the traditional curricular components, and it can be closely integrated with them. The development of such experiences—practical exposure one or two afternoons a week—should be encouraged, for they have some value and can lead to wider acceptability of full-time field experiences. For faculty members will soon recognize that, however useful such a part-time experience can be, it will invariably limit the student to the vicarious role of the *passive* observer. With this realization, the institution will be ready to explore ways in which a student can become a *participant* observer, with equal stress on the participation and on the observation.

is it education?

This article will not address the crucial question: what conditions must be fulfilled so as to make field experience *both* participation and observation; how, in other words, to make the experience not an end in itself, but a means to a better understanding—an educational experience. This question must be answered to some degree of satisfaction by the majority of faculty before field experience becomes fully accepted.

The greatest single barrier to the acceptability of experiential education among traditional faculties is the combination of their skepticism about the possibility of accomplishing this objective, together with the excessive enthusiasm of some advocates who fail to see the necessity for going beyond experience for its own sake. The most important task for the administrator who wants to bring about wider use of field experience is to emphasize, on the one hand, the importance of identifying and meeting the conditions that make the field work more than the experience alone and, on the other hand, the likelihood that in fact this goal can be achieved.

can we afford it?

The importance of the question of cost, to the institution and to the faculty member, runs a close second to that of academic respectability. There are many types and modes of field experience but all have in common that they take considerable time and effort on the part of faculty, administration, and off-campus personnel. Regardless of specific details, there are always three broad phases. Planning includes selection of field experience sites, selection and training of supervisors, and preparation of students. Supervision involves various combinations of on-the-job supervision, periodic discussions and reviews, on-going field seminars, and the like. And finally there is assessment, which again can take various forms.

Obviously a reciprocal relationship exists between these three broad aspects. The better the planning, the less the other two are needed; and the more supervision and ongoing discussion, the less post-audit assessment. Conversely, if the field experience occurred before the student's admission, the stress must be entirely on evaluation, which becomes correspondingly more difficult and time-consuming.

Time and effort carry a cost both to the institution and to the individual and must, therefore, be recognized in the reward systems which operate for the one and for the other. The operating budget for the institution must take *explicit* account of the costs of field experience. The assignment of faculty work load as well as the system of reappointments, promotions, and tenure must similarly *explicitly* recognize involvement in this mode of instruction.

The details of how this can and should be done depend on the particular circumstances at each institution—the source of operating funds; the extent to which these are based on a formula and, if so, what factors enter into this formula; whether there is a specified teaching load, and so on. Whatever the details, the conditions for proper acceptance of field work are that the costs be realistically assessed and that they be explicitly incorporated in the allocation of funds, in the assignment of work loads, and in the ways time and money are accounted for. In other words, there is here a reciprocal obligation: the institutional as well as the individual piper must insist on the necessary resources for the piping; the societal, corporate, or individual payer of the piper, in turn, can insist that the piping took place.

A fairly simple-minded example may help to show how this interlocking set of issues might be approached. Assume that extensive field work is to be introduced in an institution which is funded on the basis of a 20:1 student/faculty ratio. This context would mean that one full-time faculty member, without any other duties, should be provided for the entire task of planning, supervising, and assessing the field experience of twenty students. Assuming a twelve- to fourteen-week term, the advisor would spend six to seven hours per student in the planning phase, one hour/week per student during the term in supervision, and again six to seven hours at the end spent on assessment.

Obviously this situation can be modified in a number of ways. For example, if supervision is provided in part or entirely by adjunct, off-campus personnel (such as the actual job supervisors) the budget might carry for every twenty students a half-time faculty member in addition to half of an average faculty salary as funds for the payment of adjunct personnel. The faculty member would be expected to put in, say, half of the above total time, with a possible distribution as follows: again six to seven hours each on planning and assessment per student, and one to two hours per student spread over the entire term so as to maintain contact with the supervisors.

The example is just one of many possible models and is merely intended to show that, either working from budget formulation or working backward from the average amount of faculty and adjunct time spent on the program, it is possible to work out quite explicitly the relationship between time and cost. Such an attempt at a reasonably precise assessment must be made in order to make appropriate allowances in the institutional budget and in individual teaching and other work load assignments, as well as to state the average amount of faculty and adjunct involvement which is expected and which can therefore be insisted on by both the student and the funding source.

Having stated the need for an overall quantitive framework so as to give reasonable protection to all concerned, I must also stress the importance of maintaining maximum individual flexibility within these standards as to how much time, *on the whole* and *on the average,* should be involved in experiential instruction, just as there should not be rigid standards for traditional modes of instruction. In neither case should these be used for a time and motion type of analysis of individual faculty effort. Each faculty member or adjunct should have the maximum amount of leeway, within the overall guidelines, to work out with his students how best to conduct the field experience: Should he spend short amounts of time intensively with individual students or longer periods with larger groups? Or should more time be spent on preparing supplementary materials or on the critique of student papers and projects?

what about prior learning experience?

To accept the educational potential of field experience during a college career leads inevitably to recognizing a similar potential in prior experiences. Again the stress must be on the word *potential.* Experience, whether prior or concurrent, becomes experiential education only to the extent to which it has been digested, analyzed, and understood and can thus serve as a means to the end of illustrating and illuminating general methods and principles.

The significant difference between prior and concurrent experience is that with the former the institution and its faculty have little or no way of either planning for or supervising the field experience. Thus, the principal onus with regard to the determination of content must fall on the post-audit assessment and evaluation. Throughout this country a growing number of institutions and individuals have tackled this task and are beginning to arrive at possible approaches and processes. On the whole such auditing is still being done separately by each institution, but it is likely that the coming months will see the development of joint efforts and pooled experiences through a consortium of institutions.

Two points should be noted. First, as already indicated at the beginning of this section, the "academic respectability" of giving credit for prior experience depends, even more than the giving of credit for concurrent experience, on the explicit recognition that experience for its own sake is not enough, and that it must have served as a means toward a more general end.

Second, as in concurrent field experience, much time and effort are required on the part of the faculty, and there must be appropriate budget and work load recognition for this work. It is not possible, in the long run, to bootleg a program of assessing prior experience on the basis of voluntary faculty and institutional overload.

The difficulty in building this effort into the appropriate reward system is that one is dealing with the cost of assessing something which happened before the individual became an enrolled and tuition-paying student. Normally an institution receives little or no budgetary allowance for such processes as administering placement examinations or evaluating transfer credits, and this is justified because these are fairly mechanical procedures. However, prior experience becomes transformed into an academic equivalent only through interaction between the individual and the faculty and staff of the institution. Proper assessment means carefully preparing and analyzing a compendium of material reflecting the extent to which the prior activities have become an educational experience, and this process involves close collaboration between the applicant and one or more faculty or staff members. The academic credits, as it were, have been created through this interaction, not by the prior experience alone, and it is therefore proper that this interaction be adequately funded and rewarded, in both institutional and individual terms. This recognition is essential if academic credit for prior experience is to be widely applied.

why should we bother?

The degree of acceptability of concurrent as well as prior field experience as an integral part of the educational process will depend, when all is said and done, primarily on the degree to which traditional faculty, administrators, and public officials recognize the intrinsic need to move in this direction. It might be useful in this connection to stress two points. One has been made most cogently by Alfred North Whitehead: "*Education is the acquisition of the art of the utilization of knowledge.*" On the one hand this statement means that mere experience which is only the acquisition of undigested facts and skills is not education—but surely it also means that neither is the acquisition of knowledge without appropriate experiences to illustrate its utilization.

The second point is that, to put it quite crassly, the "clientele" for higher education will increasingly consist of persons who are returning to college after some years of job experience or national service, and even more of those who wish to pursue their education in a way which is intermixed with such off-campus activities. More and more of our students will be involved in field experience whether we like it or not; it is our great challenge to take advantage of this by transforming separate experiences into constructive experiential learning, integrated into the overall education.

reference

Schein, E. H. "Professional Education: Some New Directions." Carnegie Commission on Higher Education Profile. New York: McGraw Hill, 1972.

Ernest A. Lynton, recently appointed senior vice president for academic affairs of the University of Massachusetts, was the first dean of Livingston College at Rutgers University from 1965 to 1973.

Resources—institutions, books, films, monographs, manuals—useful in developing and improving off-campus experiential learning programs.

additional resources

john duley

The best additional resources in this field at the present time are people and operational programs. Membership in the Society for Field Experience Education provides a membership list for individual contact and the annual conference gives opportunities for personal exchange. In addition, the following annotated list of agencies, books, monographs, articles, resource manuals, and films are the things a person would find helpful in explaining Field Experience Education more fully.

books and monographs

- Zauderer, D. G. *Urban Internships in Higher Education.* ERIC/Higher Education Research Report #9. Washington, D.C.: AAHE, 1973. This is a concise, well-organized discussion of internships in which students do supervised work in governmental agencies or units and use the tools and methodology of a particular discipline to examine the institutional cultures in which they are interning. The monograph describes the goals and objectives of internship programs, discusses some problems of this model of university-based urban internships, and delineates alternative approaches to the structure and design of programs. The sections on "The System of University Values and Incentives" and the subsequent one on "Faculty Role" are very useful.

• Ritterbush, P. (Ed.) *Let the Entire Community Become Our University*. Washington, D.C.: Acropolis, 1972. Lewchuk, R. C. and Ungerer, R. (Eds.) *National Register of Internships and Experiential Education*. Washington, D.C.: Acropolis, 1973. These companion volumes were published by Acropolis in advocacy of off-campus field experience education as a means of reforming higher education, to report on existing literature, and to identify individuals and institutions engaged in this type of education. *Let the Entire Community Become Our University*, the first published, is a collection of essays written mostly by authors who are involved in field experience education in a variety of ways. Eight different types of programs are discussed in the first section. The second section presents a mix of articles, including two on cooperative education, two on new national organizations, one on the problems of evaluation, and others on the implementation of specific programs. The last four chapters are on institutional change. The book provides a valuable introduction to the rich diversity of the field.

The *National Register* is less an interpretative piece and much more of a resource book although it opens with a review of Michael Rossman's *On Learning and Social Change* and an advocacy essay arguing for a federal, community-service G. I. Bill. The rest of the volume consists of a very useful annotated cataloging of organizations, literature, and people. In the "Geography of Learning Opportunities" the editors have provided a unique service; using the zip code as an organizing tool, they list field experience education programs and the people who run them. The list includes agencies who place interns as well as college and university programs. This resource is worth the price of the book.

• Freire, P. *Pedagogy of the Oppressed*. New York: Herder and Herder, 1970. This is a hard-hitting analysis and criticism of traditional education as a tool of the oppressor which continues the enslavement of the oppressed by stifling the human spirit through its "banking" tradition (the depositing of knowledge in the mind of the learner). The author, an educator and philosopher, presents a philosophy of education built on mutual involvement. The learning process is a two-way street in which all parties learn together and from each other. He speaks out of the experience of radical educational involvement with the oppressed and the book rings with authenticity. It is the best description of what the relationship ought to be between students and faculty in field experience education.

• Harrison, R., and Hopkins, R. "An Alternative to the Univesity Model." *Journal of Applied Behavioral Science,* 1967, *3*(4). The article is a report on the authors' experiences in training people for the Peace Corps using a cross-cultural learning model. They provide an excellent description of and comparison between the goals and metagoals of traditional university education and cross-cultural education as well as insights into the importance and value of the latter.

• Raths, L. E., Harmin, M., and Simon, S. B. *Values and Teaching.* Columbus: Charles E. Merrill, 1966. Simon, S. B., and others. *Values Clarification.* New York: Hart, 1972. Both of these books were written for use by public school teachers but they are helpful in understanding the process of using values in decision making and in suggesting exercises or strategies for exploring values with students. The first describes the valuing process and the rationale for being concerned with this in the schools. The second volume is devoted to exercises developed and used by teachers in clarifying values.

institutions

A valuable additional resource is the National Center for Public Service Internship Programs, founded in 1972 to help universities and public organizations advance internship programs. It promotes the establishment and acceptance of internships, disseminates information, carries out research and offers technical assistance, represents internship interests in the national capital, and promotes new revenues for supporting internship programs. It publishes an excellent newsletter as a vehicle for accomplishing these objectives. Each issue includes information on new developments in service-learning internships and on relevant legislation before the Congress. Each newsletter also contains an article reporting on research or a point of view by an educator or placement agency person involved in an internship program. Individual membership, which costs $15 yearly, includes a subscription to the Newsletter. The address is Suite 201, 1140 Connecticut Ave., N.W., Washington, D.C. 20036.

placement opportunities

Identifying and making available to students information about acceptable placements for specific academic programs is a problem each field education program has to solve. It requires individualized solutions because the purposes and objectives of each program are distinctive and its placement needs are therefore unique. A national data bank has been proposed from time to time but the diversity among programs and the multitude of agencies, organizations, and opportunities, each having a very limited number of placements, makes such a venture impractical. Each program develops its own network of placements depending on its own specific needs. There are some standard resources which are widely used especially by programs which are flexible about what is acceptable for field experience education and which encourage student initiative in designing and creating projects. The most widely used of these resources are:

- Cavener, James N. (Ed.) *Invest Yourself.* New York: The Commission on Voluntary Service and Action (475 Riverside Drive, Room 665, New York, New York, 10027), 63 pgs., $1.00 per single copy. This is a yearly listing of summer and some year-round service opportunities provided primarily by churches and religious organizations, although other agencies are also included. These opportunities are listed according to the type of service and by age of volunteer desired, either high school or college.
- Cohen, M. A. *The Whole World Handbook, Six Continents on a Student Budget, Travel, Study, Work.* New York: Frommer/Pasmantier and Council on International Educational Exchange (777 United Nations Plaza, New York, New York 10017), $3.50 paper. This book describes study and work opportunities as well as travel and inexpensive sleeping and eating accommodations in Eastern and Western Europe, the Middle East, Africa, Asia, Latin America, Canada, Australia, New Zealand, and the U.S.S.R. It is an excellent resource for students creating their own projects overseas and those on established programs who will be doing some independent traveling.
- The Center for Curriculum Design. *Somewhere Else, A Living-Learning Catalog.* Chicago: Swallow Press (P.O. Box 350, Evanston, Illinois 60204), 1972, $3.00 paper. "For young adults seeking an alternative to college, and older adults who seek continued meaningful learning situations unencumbered by formal academic requirements and procedures."
- Vocations for Social Change (4911 Telegraph Ave., Oakland, California, 94609). *Work Force.* Sample copy $1.00, subscription $5.00 for six months. This is a bimonthly publication providing feature articles about alternative life styles and occupations and a major section of Job Listings, Proposals and News. In this section they describe placement opportunities under such headings as Alternative Institutions, Education/Research, Media, and Organizing. This

resource is useful for students arranging their own placements and creating their own projects.

• The most complete local resource center in the U.S.A. is C/AHED, the Center for Alternatives in and for Higher Education, developed and operated by the United Ministries in Higher Education at Michigan State University under the directorship of Donald Ward. C/AHED exists for the purpose of helping people get in touch with themselves and the world through real and tangible experiences. It is supported by a collective of Michigan State University and off-campus units that seek to provide resources for those who are serious about alternative educational experience for a summer, a term or two, or a year or longer. It provides information about voluntary social service, educational alternatives, travel, and part-time employment. The Center plans to publish, with the aid of a Danforth Foundation Kenneth Underwood Grant, a book describing the resource, how it was created and is kept up to date, managed, and utilized. The purpose of the book is to aid those desiring to create similar resources in their own communities. The publication date is fall of 1975. Mr. Ward's address is United Ministries in Higher Education, 1118 S. Harrison Road, East Lansing, Mich., 48823.

films

Two 16 mm color films were produced for the 1973 conference of the Society for Field Experience Education. One film describes the practices of the Georgia Intern Program as it functions through the office responsible for the statewide program, and the other, entitled "More Able Persons," describes the campus-based program at Mars Hill College in Mars Hill, North Carolina. These films are a good general introduction to and interpretation of field experience education, especially in reference to the service-learning internship model. The Georgia film is available from Mr. Michael Hart, Georgia Intern Office, Office of the Governor, State Capitol, Atlanta, Georgia, 30334. The film on Mars Hill College is available through Mr. Robert Sigmon, North Carolina Internship Office, 116 W. Jones Street, Raleigh, North Carolina, 27603.

program manuals

These have been developed by many program directors for use by their own staff and students and may be useful to those who are initiating new programs. Program directors are usually very willing to share these resources with others upon request. One nationally produced manual which is well done and has wider useability than the purpose for which it was intended is: Corey, K. and Stuart, A. *Community Internships for Undergraduate Geography Students,* Washington, D.C.: Association of American Geographers (1710 Sixteenth St., N.W., 20009), 10 pps, 1973. This pamphlet is subtitled "Guidelines for Internship Programs" and is a Consulting Services Publication of the Commission on College Geography of the Association. It gives a rationale for such programs and describes a model for a large internship operation covering the three major areas of program planning, implementation, and evaluation. It would be useful to anyone planning to develop a new field experience education program of any kind.

evaluation

One of the pressing issues in field experience education is what methods to use in evaluating student learning. In addition to a clear statement of specific objectives for each program, the means of assessment need to be developed and refined. Educational Testing Service has received a grant from the Carnegie Foundation to create and validate evaluative methods for experiential education. They have initiated the Cooperative Assessment of Experiential Learning project (CAEL) under the directorship of Warren Willingham. They began their work in the spring of 1974 and are asking institutions to assist them in developing and testing methods of evaluation. Interested persons should correspond with Dr. Willingham, Educational Testing Service, Princeton, N.J., 08540.

Lemke, W. H. Jr. "The Individual Opinion Inventory: A Progress Report on the Assessment of Off-Campus and Overseas Study Programs." *Critique: A Quarterly Memorandum* (The Center for the Study of Higher Education, The University of Toledo, Toledo, Ohio, 43606), 1974, *6*(1), 4 pps. This issue reports the progress that has been made through phase one and into phase two of the design and validation of a research instrument (IOI) for assessing changes in students' attitudes and character development affected by study off campus. While apparently prepared for use primarily with students engaged in formal academic study programs overseas or off campus, the instrument is designed to collect and analyze information about changes in the affective domain of students who study away from school and so should be useful in field experience education programs. Phase two, which started this spring, will consist of the rigorous and systematic collection of pre- and post-data on the IOI and further, more detailed investigations of affective changes which are attributable to study off campus.

index